The Hidden Power of Dreams

The HIDDEN POWER of DREAMS

How to Use Dreams on Your Spiritual Journey

DENISE LINN

(Previously titled: *Pocketful of Dreams*)

BALLANTINE BOOKS • NEW YORK

Copyright © 1988 by Denise Linn

All rights reserved under International and Pan-American Copyright Conventions. Published in the United States by Ballantine Books, a division of Random House, Inc., New York, and distributed in Canada by Random House of Canada Limited, Toronto. Originally published under the title *Pocketful of Dreams* in somewhat different form in Australia in 1988 by Triple Five Publishing, a division of Nacson and Sons Pty. Ltd., and in Great Britain in 1993 by Judy Piatkus (Publishers) Ltd.

http://www.randomhouse.com

Library of Congress Catalog Card Number: 97-93661

ISBN: 0-345-40003-8

Cover design by Min Choi
Cover photo © Telegraph Colour Library/FPG International
Text design by Ann Gold

Manufactured in the United States of America

First American Edition: August 1997

10   9   8   7   6   5   4   3   2   1

*This book is dedicated to David,
the "man of my dreams,"
and to Meadow,
my dream child.*

CONTENTS

INTENT

Each of us is on a quest, a journey that carries us through time and space. Your quest has led you to this book and it will continue to lead you through your personal evolution. The purpose of this book is to show you how your dreams can help you penetrate the realm beyond your physical senses to gain answers to your deepest questions and help you reach self-knowledge. My intent is to provide information that will allow you to discover your own internal answers, which are not found in anyone's teachings but are woven within your feelings, within the patterns of your life and within your dreams.

ACKNOWLEDGMENTS

Thank you, Leon Nacson, for having the dream that inspired this book. You are a profound visionary in every sense of the word and a wonderful friend.

Ann Sewell, it was your unwavering dedication that took this book to its completion. Your willingness to consistently and undauntedly persevere will always be an inspiration to me. You brought this book to life.

To the Computer Mystic and Agent of Fortune, Karl Bettinger, I give my sincere thanks.

Thanks, Barb Kelly! You made creating this book so much fun. Who would think typing copy could be funny?

Jane Bakkan, as your long-awaited child grew within you, your gentle magic helped give birth to this book. Thank you.

Barbara Roper, your quiet wisdom warmed many late nights.

Alice Allen, thank you for guiding us softly down the path of graciousness.

Lydia Christofides, thank you for your remarkable insights.

Anne Sweet, your poems carried us on dream wings of the night.

Thanks, Cheryl Steinle, for your steadfast dedication.

Phillip Crockford, you are always part of our family. Thanks for your help.

Thank you, Ken Colbung (Nundjan Djiridjakin), spiritual leader and senior male clan leader of the Australian Aborigine Bibulmun tribe, for your insights and support.

To Glynn Braddy, I'm glad you are in our life.

Much thanks to Dancing Feather, friend and teacher. You are never far from my heart.

The Hidden Power of Dreams

THE BEGINNING

*D*reams are the mysterious language of the night. Each evening after the setting sun has beckoned the moon, a golden harvest is woven into our slumbering consciousness. Visions from this enigmatic, nocturnal realm have been described as messages from the gods and have helped shape the destiny of individuals as well as nations. Since the dawn of time, dream weavers have slipped through the crack between the two worlds to touch the reaches of inner space and reap the harvest of the night.

These secret messages from the mind can foretell your future, reveal your past, and warn you of danger. They can contain creative inspiration or assist in melting the barriers in your life. Dreams can serve as a doorway to the mystic arena of the night for inner-dimensional travel and communication on the inner realms with loved ones. They can be a springboard for night healing, astral travel, and soul searching.

But we have forgotten.

Dreams are now but relics of the mind. We can no longer call on the Muses of the Night by direct path.

In ancient times, when the cycles of nature and the cycles of man were closely intertwined, dreams of the past and the future, dreams of hunting and planting, and those of war and peace all directed the course of the tribe or culture. Dreams were a natural outflow originating from a deep alignment with the forces of nature. In those night hours, emissaries of nighttime wisdom were called on to send forth inner truths.

But we have forgotten.

It has become commonplace to consider sleep as a time when we do nothing "productive." We acknowledge the reality of dreams; however, even if we recall our dreams, they are rarely considered valuable or imperative to our well-being, as are the *real* events of the day.

When our children have nightmares, we comfort them with "It's only a dream," casually tossing aside a remarkable communication from the depths of their being. At best, dreams are viewed as an inner "data processing" of the mind.

But the time has come to remember. We are passing through a crucial period on our planet. It will become increasingly important to awaken the dreamer within each of us and listen to the oracle of the heart so that we may step lightly through the times ahead.

My Dream Journey

My journey into the realm of dreams began on an early summer afternoon more than twenty years ago in the Midwest. It was a glorious day, with golden summer haze dusting the fields. Amber swirls of wheat and honey-colored corn tassels sailed by on either side of me as I joyously drove my motor bike down the back roads of our rural farming community. I was seventeen years old. Suddenly, the silken serenity of that summer day was shattered by a sniper's bullet. I was left for dead by an unknown assailant. In that one shattering instant, my life and all that was familiar to me spun crazily; when it settled, I knew I would never be the same again. A passing farmer summoned an ambulance.

As I lay in the emergency room, struggling with the searing

pain that racked my entire body, I became conscious of the pain subsiding and being enveloped by a quiet stillness, and then blackness . . . velvet-soft, gentle blackness. Was I dead? I felt as if I were encased in a black bubble. Then suddenly the bubble burst and I was bathed in brilliant light. It was a most peculiar experience—I *was* the light. I was an all-pervading luminescent light. I became aware of a sweet, pure music that wafted through the universe. It ebbed and flowed like waves of liquid light. It was more exquisite than any symphony I had ever heard. An undulating harmony pervaded me until I became the music. In that moment it seemed I was made only of light and sound. There was nothing that was not me. I had no sense of time, no past or future. Everything just *was*.

Something about that place felt very familiar. It was as if I had been there before. In each of us resides an intuitive sense of love that is as natural as breathing. This love goes beyond all boundaries, beyond form, like an unlimited ocean pene-trating every cell and molecule of our being. I felt a deep inner awareness of this kind of love. It wasn't the type of love that you can fall "into" or "out of." There was no separation, no "me-ness" or "you-ness," in this love. It just was.

I felt as if I had come home. Then suddenly a deep and powerful voice declared, "You may not stay here. There is something that you still need to do." I shouted, "Nooo!" as I was pulled back into my body.

I later discovered that my experience was very similar to what many individuals describe as a "near-death" experience. These individuals often report seeing a bright light and feeling extraordinary peace and usually a vague sense of familiarity. Regardless of how you define what happened to me, it changed my perception of reality forever.

My near-death experience was completely foreign to me. I was the eldest of four children, and both my parents had spent time in the scientific community. My father was an engineer, and my mother, who was of Native American descent, had worked as a chemist. Growing up I thought the only things that were real, were those that were tangible and provable by the laws of science. Now, I struggled to find a way to fit my near-death experience into my beliefs about the nature of reality. Instead, I found that slowly, everything in which I had believed began to disintegrate. In its place, a new understanding began to emerge. It seemed my life was to take an entirely new direction.

As I recovered from my injuries, my dreams began to take on a particular vividness and significance. In addition, I began to hear music that no one else could hear, and I was often aware of very loving spirit beings surrounding me. Somehow, my brush with death had allowed me to stumble into inner dimensions long forgotten. This was all very strange to me, with my very rational, linear approach to life.

Another astonishing revelation was the awareness that "I" was separate from my body. "I" was not my body. As a result of the shooting, I lost my spleen, an adrenal gland, a kidney, and had damage to my stomach and intestines, lung, and diaphragm, and I now had a tube replacing the aorta out of my heart. My body was damaged, but "I" was not. To me, this was an amazing realization, and it began to assist me greatly in the healing of my body. I became extraordinarily healthy in spite of my injuries.

As time passed, I found that my dreams were not always idyllic. Somehow, when that nocturnal portal of perception opened for me, images that had been held back for so long surged forward en masse, with extraordinary dreams of bright colors and intensity. Often the images were terrifying; others were profoundly soothing and reassuring. In my dreams I would occasionally catch a fleeting glimpse of that place to which I had traveled when I was thought to have died. I would clutch at these cloudy images, only to find them vanishing like mist. I longed to return, but I wasn't willing to die to get there.

During this time I frequently dreamed of a shadowy figure chasing me. I would often wake too terrified to return to sleep. This foreboding, formless creature of the night continued to haunt my dreams through the next few years.

I began a career in journalism, and in the summer of 1969 I was in Eastern Europe attending a journalism conference. At its culmination, I decided to camp on one of the numerous islands off the coast of what was then Yugoslavia. I persuaded a very reluctant fisherman to take me to a beautiful deserted island. As I lay in my sleeping bag that first night, I looked up at the ceiling of the night and lost myself in the loneliness of the stars. God seemed so close, yet so very far away.

The next morning, the sun-dappled stillness was invaded by a plane flying low overhead—too low, I thought. Without warning, I was showered with a rain of gunfire! Bullets were everywhere, ricocheting off rocks and trees. I dived for cover, crawling under some bushes for safety while the shooting continued. And then, just as suddenly as it began, it stopped. As I crept out from beneath the bushes, a black terror filled me.

Why was I being shot at again? Was I there to delve into a deeper understanding of self? I didn't understand.

Within a short time, I was able to flag down a passing fisherman, who, in broken English, explained that no one should have taken me to that island in the first place. It was off limits because it was sometimes used for aerial target practice.

In my dreams, my shadowy pursuer increased his nightly rampage.

Later that year, I returned to the United States. The newspaper for which I worked sent me to cover anti–Vietnam War riots in the cities of Chicago, New York, and Washington, D.C. I recall being on the front line of a march in Washington, D.C., when policemen with gas masks and billy clubs exploded into the street from every direction, shooting tear gas and pepper gas into the front line of the march. These exceedingly painful and noxious gases feel as if they are searing your eyes and skin. Canisters of gas exploded at my feet. Added to the din were the screams of the panicked crowd. I watched as people near me, unable to match the force of the crowd, were swept under the feet of those desperately trying to flee from the gas.

As tumultuous as my daylight hours were, my nights were even more terrifying. My vigilant assailant of the night continued to hound me like a wolf on the scent of an impending kill. To hold at bay the tenacious grip of my midnight pursuer, I used my daylight hours to enhance my willingness to face "danger." To compensate for my fear, I tested my mettle with karate lessons and skydiving. At the same time, my work was filled with the violence associated with reporting riots and confrontations. I even had to fend off the attack of a knife-wielding rapist.

Shortly after that attack, serendipity decreed that a book on Zen Buddhism would reach me. I was impressed with the remarkable similarity between my near-death experience and the content of the book. It talked of the Great Light and the feeling of oneness with all things. It spoke of going beyond linear time. I wondered if it was possible to reach that place again without dying. I knew that it was time for a change in my life. The time had come for me to follow my heart path, to search for that vital perception I had encountered when I was shot.

Expecting to stay only a short time, I moved into a Zen monastery in the early 1970s. My brief visit stretched into over two years. During much of this time, I gazed at a wall four to sixteen hours a day, sitting in a full or half-lotus position. In a Zen monastery it is easy to be distracted by pain or tiredness. So, as an act of compassion, the Zen master would hit the shoulder of a Zen practitioner with a *kyôsaku* stick to ensure attentiveness in his discipline. A *kyôsaku* stick is similar to a flat baseball bat. The blow landing excruciatingly on my shoulder would seem to reverberate off the monastery walls. The catch-22 of this practice was that if the Zen master deemed that I was doing really well, he would smack as hard as he could with the *kyōsaku* in order to encourage me.

Visions would come to me and the Zen master would say, "Only illusions . . . Go deeper." Great insights would come and the Zen master would say, "Only illusions. Keep going. Go for the underlying reality . . . the true reality. See yourself as you really are." These words would be echoed by a recurring theme in my future life.

As I stayed on in the Zen monastery, my dreams began to change. In one, a radiant, three-dimensional, animated mandala appeared. A mandala is a symbolic pattern divided into four sections, usually found within a circle or square, thought to represent the universe. When I inquired into the spontaneous appearance, I was told that Carl Jung believed mandalas were dream symbols that heralded wholeness. Jung indicated that the universal occurrence of the number four (four directions, a square with four sides, a mandala with four sides) promoted wholeness and self-integration.

While I was living in the monastery, I made a discovery concerning the nightly antagonist of my dreams. As I was once again chased down a labyrinth of shadowy corridors, I stopped abruptly and thought, "This is only a dream. I'm going to face whoever is chasing me." As I did so, my nemesis became a nebulous form slinking away into the shadows. Though the nightly appearances continued, as I turned and faced my pursuer each time, it would disappear without revealing its face. (See chapter 9.)

My Zen training made me aware that there were ways to heal my body from within.

It was during this time that I met a Hawaiian kahuna, or shaman, who was a great healer. She allowed me to consciously glimpse the inner realms that I had been exploring randomly in my dreams. She agreed to train me only after she discovered my Native American heritage. This wise woman opened the doors of my understanding so that I could see how Spirit resides in everything, and how one can call on Spirit for healing. I recall an occasion when I took her to Jackass Ginger, a tropical forest in Hawaii, so that she might present fruit to the menehune king. (Menehunes are Hawaiian elves.) As I stood lingering at the forest's edge, I was struck with how incredible it was that I was with someone who was talking with *elves*. For the kahuna, the boundaries between the dream state and the waking state were blurred, and one could step lightly between the two worlds.

During my training with the kahuna, I began to recognize an entirely new dimension of dreaming. I discovered that I could leave my body, walk around my cottage, and even turn to look at my sleeping body. (See chapter 13.) The visits of my nightly tormentor became fewer and fewer during this time. Though the visits were not as terrifying, I was still unable to view the face, and the lingering shadow continued to haunt me.

I wanted to understand as much as I could about my inner potential, so I began to study with various teachers. Among those who would touch me deeply was a diminutive Japanese woman, Hawayo Takata. When we met, she said that she had been waiting for me and asked what had taken me so long. She was the individual who brought Reiki from Japan to the west, and she taught me to access the life force energy so that it would surge down my arms in my healing work. I eventually organized her first courses for westerners.

Another teacher, an eccentric shiatsu master, shared the wisdom of balancing the body through pressure points, those exquisite points of intergalactic synchronization.

As I further explored the healing realm, I was asked to teach healing through the University of Hawaii Continuing Education Program. Thus began my vocation as a teacher.

During this time an elusive waft of masculine serenity and

strength began to drift into my dreams. Floating images of a tall, shrouded man would emanate from the shadows of the midnight hours. Who was this pleasant intruder? I made a list of the characteristics of this dream lover, and it turned out to include all I had ever wanted in a lover and companion.

Two weeks after I made this list, I was attending a self-growth communication course. I was dissatisfied with the course and raised my hand to share this with the instructor. Rather than deal with my questions, he apparently thought that what I really needed was something to keep me busy. His response was "So, why don't you marry that guy sitting next to you?" Feeling very irritated, I said to the tall, serene man next to me, "Will you marry me?" To my utter amazement, he said, "Yes!" (I knew this individual but I wasn't dating him.)

I felt shaky as I realized that I had just asked someone to marry me. The instructor began to goad me as to when the momentous event would take place. Finally, I said petulantly, "Okay, I'll get married tomorrow." My logical, conscious mind thought, "This is completely absurd," but a gentle tugging welled up from deep within my subconscious mind . . . a gentle remembering. That vague, benevolent phantom shape that had recently appeared in my dreams began a metamorphosis into the man sitting next to me—the man who would become my husband, the man of my dreams.

After our marriage, the most remarkable thing happened. I dreamed that my tormentor was chasing me again! This time, when I turned to face my fear, I was shocked. It was me! It had always been me. In that moment I embraced this lonely waif who had chased me for so long. I felt as if I were coming home. And in my coming home, a child was conceived and born to David and me. As a result of my injuries, the doctors had told me I could never have children. So the child was a miracle to me. I had a healthy, easy home birth. Our daughter, Meadow, has grown into a lovely child. Being a mother has been perhaps my greatest "teacher" of all.

This book is a culmination of twenty years of self-exploration. Through many dramatic and often painful experiences, I have been beckoned to come closer to understanding myself through my dreams. May this book help you gain self-knowledge through your dreams, in safety and joy. Thank you for allowing me to participate in your life.

Dream Gates

Come into my dream garden,
Across the bridge of sleep . . .

1.

WHAT SCIENTISTS SAY ABOUT DREAMS

Experimenting,
I hung the moon
on various
branches of the pine
    —Hokushi

*I*magine a resplendent garden surrounded by a wall with many gates. As you enter from the eastern gate, you view tall, golden-tasseled corn gently undulating in the warm breeze. Ripe, full grapes hang on the vines, and giant tomatoes radiate their sweet fragrance. Ah, you think, this is surely a garden of nourishment and sustenance.

Entering from the southern gate, you see rich, black soil. A pungent smell permeates the warm air. This garden is the fertile ground that seeds new beginnings, a place of regeneration and renewal.

The western gate swings open to reveal a magic carpet of dahlias, cosmos, sunflowers, daisies, and marigolds. A symphony of color envelops you in a warm blanket of spring. This is an exquisite flower garden, a cathedral of rare beauty.

The same garden . . . different gates.

13

Each gate offers a new and varied perception. There are various "gates" through which you can enter your garden of dreams.

Stepping through the well-worn gate of science, the verdant rows of new growth are neat and orderly, each carefully tended and numbered. Scientists believe that dreaming is an activity in which we all participate. Research indicates that *everyone* dreams. Even blind people dream. Individuals with an extremely low IQ have no fewer dreams than those possessing a high IQ. Dreaming is as natural a process as breathing. There is no way, with the exception of drug use or overindulgence in alcohol, that dreaming can be prevented.

Though we can experience as few as three or as many as nine, we average four to five dreams per night. Those who claim they don't dream actually have difficulty only in remembering their dreams. In fact, each of us spends approximately 20 percent of our total sleep time dreaming. On average, we dream for about an hour and a half each night. Over a lifetime, we spend as much time dreaming as it takes to get an advanced university education. Yet, researchers really know very little about dreams.[1]

What researchers do know is that during the dream state, the heartbeat speeds up or slows down for no discernible reason. The blood pressure climbs and dives unpredictably. The pulse becomes irregular, as does the breathing pattern. Metabolism increases, and the kidneys produce less but more concentrated urine. Spontaneous firing of brain cells is sometimes increased beyond normal waking levels. Blood flow to the brain increases 40 percent. Smaller muscles such as those in the fingers tend to twitch, while larger muscles go limp.

REM Sleep

Dreams usually occur during REM sleep, which refers to rapid eye movement. REM sleep was discovered in the early

1950s. Until that time, most scientists even remotely interested in the sleep state agreed with the renowned Russian
physiologist Ivan Pavlov, who believed that the brain sort of
"tuned down" during sleep. Then, Dr. Nathan Kleitman, a
professor of physiology at the University of Chicago, and
considered the father of modern sleep research, requested that
one of his graduate students, Eugene Aserinski, help him
investigate the relationship between eye movement and sleep.
Aserinski and Kleitman discovered that if they woke someone
while his eyes were still moving rapidly from side to side and
asked what was being experienced, the person would almost
always say that he was in the middle of a dream. This
discovery had amazing impact on the scientific community, which could now begin the research and study of dream
phenomena.[2]

During REM sleep, vivid images in the brain issue com-
mands to jump, run, or kick. Movement of the eyes in various
directions corresponds with the type of action reported by the
dreamer. These action-oriented messages are countermanded
by neurons in the brain stem that disconnect much of our
muscular apparatus, so we are effectively paralyzed during the
dream state. When this area of the brain stem has been damaged, people have been known to act out their dreams dramatically, sometimes to the extent that they may need to be
tied to their beds so as not to injure themselves or others.[3]

REM states generally repeat in ninety-minute cycles. A
ninety-minute cycle of non-REM sleep usually occurs when
we first drift off to sleep. Our brain waves then begin to put on
a remarkable display as the sleeper begins the first REM period
of the night. When awakened during the night a person may
not be able to go back to sleep until one complete ninety-
minute sleep session has been missed. The average sleeper has
four or five REM periods per night. These periods each begin
with a very short REM period of ten minutes and end in the
early morning with a dream period of 30 to 45 minutes. Some

scientists say that dreaming refreshes the cortex (the outer layer of the brain) by clearing overloaded circuits. This means that dreams are considered an electrochemical process to clear away unusable data collected during the day.[4]

Dreams and Twins

Experiments in France suggest that genetics plays some role in the phenomenon of dreaming. Research using identical twins reflects an unusual similarity in REM patterns, one far greater than that between ordinary siblings. In fact, identical twins share the same timing and duration of their REM periods. These French scientists believe that the portion of the brain that controls the dream state is governed by heredity. They go on to note instances where twins have had the same dream on the same night. However, perceiving the dream garden from a different gate, a metaphysician would explain that twins have the same dream because they are psychically connected. Current scientific investigation into clairvoyant and precognitive dreams proposes that the experiences and emotions of our ancestors are contained in our DNA and RNA through genetic coding.[5]

Necessity of Dreams

Even if we do not recall our dreams, they are necessary to our emotional and physical balance. Deprived of our dream states, we have difficulty concentrating and become nervous and edgy. Without REM sleep, in some instances, there are psychotic symptoms and hallucinations.[6]

It used to be thought that insomnia was harmful because it deprived us of the activity of sleep. It is now realized that insomnia is harmful because it deprives us of dreams as well. Great personality disturbances result from dream deprivation. Few people can endure more than seventy-two hours without dreaming. Subjects who persevere finally begin to experience hallucinations. The mind appears to create its own stimulation in the form of fantasy when the normal channels of stimulation are cut off. One of the dangers of alcohol is that it has been proven to shorten dream time. When an alcoholic withdraws from addiction, almost 100 percent of his or her sleep time is spent dreaming. This is because the person who does not dream recovers REM sleep on subsequent nights in the exact amount of time as that lost during previous nights' deprivation. Interestingly, deprivation of non-REM sleep does not appear to create a need to make up for lost sleep. Perhaps the body, in its wisdom, knows something that the mind has not yet begun to comprehend.[7]

Hypnogogic Dreams

Not technically defined as a REM dream, the hypnogogic dream belongs to the mysterious realm between wakefulness and dreaming. It is characterized by quick, random hallucinations that often take the form of faces or country scenes. Each can continue for a significant period of time.[8]

Scientists do not consider these "true dreams" because you remain consciously aware of all that is going on around you. The scientific view is that these are simply memory pictures clearing from the brain. However, a metaphysical perspective would be that during hypnogogic dreaming, the mind acts much like a radio flipping randomly among stations. The various stations are thoughts, feelings, and images that other people have had in the past, present, and future. This type of dreaming reflects a random tuning in to different realities.

Children and Dreams

Research indicates that REM sleep may be related to brain development. Premature newborns spend as much as 75 percent of their sleep time in REM, while in normal newborns that rate is around 50 percent. Five-year-olds typically spend 25 to 30 percent of their sleep time in REM. By adolescence, the rate is about 20 percent, which is typical for most adults as well. In older adults—age sixty and older—the rate drops to about 15 percent. The content of dreams changes as well with increasing age. Young children dream of many animals, such as tigers, lions, snakes, and spiders. (See chapter 27.) With increasing age, they dream less and less about animals, until adulthood, when such dreams occur less than 8 percent of the time.[9]

Animals and Dreams

You might have noticed your cat or dog showing signs of REM when their eyes twitch or their breathing becomes irregular during sleep. This has led researchers to hypothesize that most animals do, in fact, dream. Reptiles and snakes, however, have never been shown to dream, even though they spend some 60 percent of their time asleep. Interestingly, if you separate mammals into two groups, the hunted (rabbits, sheep, deer, elk, etc.) and the hunter (dogs, cats, man, etc.), the hunters usually spend 20 to 25 percent of their sleep time dreaming. The hunted sleep less with only 6 to 8 percent of their sleep time spent in dreaming.[10]

Research with animals suggests that dreaming must have an essential evolutionary value. There is no single mammal that does not dream, with the exception of the dolphin, which possesses an unusual sleep pattern. Instead of REM sleep, dolphins sleep with only half of their brain at a time. I believe that the dolphin may be the keeper of a secret of sleep. To the advanced yogi, there is very little difference between the dream state and the wakeful state. Perhaps the dolphin has unwittingly dissolved the dream boundaries at the cellular level.[11]

Dream-Inspired Scientific Discoveries

While scientific dream research and investigation continue, many scientific discoveries have been dream inspired. Descartes, the man who first postulated Rational Empiricism, came upon his theory as a result of a vivid dream. Rational Empiricism is the theory underlying the development of modern science.[12]

The man who understood the molecular structure of benzine made his discovery as a result of dreaming of a snake biting its tail. This resulted in the ring-like shape of molecular structure. He once counseled his fellow colleagues, "Gentlemen, learn to dream!" Einstein, when asked about the inspiration for his theory of relativity, replied that it came from a dream during his youth. In this dream he was riding on a sled, and as the sled sped faster and faster, it seemed to approach the speed of light. The stars were distorted and transformed into astonishing colors and patterns. In that moment, Einstein was profoundly aware of the immense power of this transformation. He related that not only did this dream inspire his theory of relativity but that his entire scientific career could be seen as an extended meditation on that particular dream.[13]

Niels Bohr, the man who developed the theory of the structure of the atom, based his theory on a dream. He dreamed he was at the races. As he observed the marked lanes on the track within which the horses were running, he constructed the analogy of fixed and specific orbits of electrons circulating around the atomic nuclei. This led to the formulation of his quantum theory, for which he later won the Nobel Prize.[14]

In the middle of the nineteenth century, a man named Elias Howe had been working for some time to invent a machine that could sew. He tried one design after another, but none was successful in stitching layers of fabric together. One day, in complete despair, he fell asleep at his work. He was rapidly plunged into a nightmare in which he was pursued and captured by a savage group of African warriors. They tied him up and poked at him with their spears. Howe awoke feeling very upset. He was unable to get back to work or dispel the vivid images of the dream from his mind. He could still clearly see the warriors' odd spears. Strange blades were tied to the ends of the long sticks—the ends of the points were perforated by a hole. That was it! A needle with a hole in the end of it! Howe immediately set to work and came up with the basic design for the first successful sewing machine. His original design is still used for all sewing machines. Mass production of clothing became possible for the first time in history. Howe solved the impasse in his invention through creative dreaming.[15]

2.

WHAT PSYCHOLOGISTS SAY ABOUT DREAMS

*T*o a psychologist, dreams are more than an electro-chemical process. Each one is a precious seed that can be nurtured and fertilized so that it will sprout, grow, and bloom to give fullness and understanding to our waking hours.

Therapists feel that dreams are the secret portal through which the psyche pours vital information into consciousness as a way to keep emotional balance during waking life. Dreams are a way for us to work out the difficulties that are suppressed rather than experienced during the day.

In my private healing practice, I've discovered that it isn't always the traumas that we *have* experienced that block us. It is often the traumas or difficulties that we *did not* allow our-selves to experience fully that create barriers in our lives. Dreams can be one way to release those barriers.

Once, in Hawaii, when I had hurt my foot running into a large stump, my mentor, the kahuna, told me to put my foot against it and put the pain back into the base of the tree. As I put my foot against the stump, I was astonished to feel a release of pain and a soothing wave of relaxation fill my foot. I thought it was kahuna magic. In a primordial way, it made sense. The tree stump had given me the pain, so I gave it back.

When I mentioned this incident to a psychologist friend, he said, "You're so dumb! You can't put pain back into a tree stump. What you were doing was allowing yourself to experience the pain that you were suppressing. By reenacting the situation that caused you the pain in the first place—by putting your foot to the stump—you felt and released what you didn't allow yourself to feel when it first happened. By suppressing physical or emotional pain, you sustain it. When you allow yourself to feel totally and completely or become 'one' with your pain, there is no separation between you and it. It disappears."

To relive is to relieve. Dreams are a safe way to relive and relieve the feelings and sensations that you don't process or experience during the day. You can use your dreams to release barriers in your wakeful hours.

Dream Analysts

Psychological study of dreams has its roots in the late 1800s. In 1861, a therapist named Scherner brought forth the idea that daytime objects or emotions could be objectified in a dream. For example, lungs could be seen as balloons and anger could become a raging fire.[1]

In 1877, Strümpell, another dream explorer, stated that dreams were escape mechanisms. They were a way to avoid experiencing the world. He formulated the Law of Association, and from this Freud's theory of association of ideas evolved. Another theory explored during this time was that the function of dreams was similar to that of our eliminative processes. Their purpose was to rid us of useless thoughts. Dreams were also theorized as being signs of wish fulfillment. Other analysts believed that dreams were memories from childhood, or complexes, or sexual desires, but it was Freud who united the different theories into a viable therapy.[2]

SIGMUND FREUD

Freud (1856–1939) encouraged his patients to talk at length about their dreams. He suggested that they notice the thoughts that the dreams evoked. His technique of free association of ideas evolved from working with his patients in this way. Freud felt that dreams were a form of repression or wish fulfillment or both. He felt that a person could reach walled-up emotions only through free association. Even dreams with painful contents were analyzed as fulfillment dreams. He divided the psyche into three parts: the ego, the id, and the superego. The ego reflects our conscious self, the id is associated with our primitive instincts, and the superego represents our social conditioning.[3]

Freud thought that during sleep, the ego was absent and the id—our basic primordial needs for sex and survival—came forth. To protect the ego and the superego from these sexual desires, the id camouflaged them by producing symbolic dreams in the hope of preventing a shock to the dreamer. The function of a dream, in Freud's theory, was to preserve sleep. Therefore, our irrational wishes were disguised as other things to deceive our self-censoring superego. Freud viewed dreams as a compromise between the suppressing forces of the id and the repressing forces of the superego. Dreams were a code to be figured out. Freudian symbolic language was very narrow, for it mostly concerned our primitive desires. The vast majority of Freudian symbols were disguises for the various forms of the sexual drive. Freud felt that even if the experiences during the day triggered dreams, their primary energy came from a childhood experience usually regarding sexual frustration.[4]

CARL JUNG

Swiss psychologist Carl Jung, an associate of Freud, found the Freudian approach rather limiting. Jung felt that the sexual drive was important but was not the determining factor in dreams. In Jung's approach, a dream object could be exactly what it was. A snake could be just a snake; it wasn't always a phallic symbol. Jung focused on the actual form of a dream rather than branch off into free association. He felt that there was no censor at work in the mind. Dreams were revelations of the unconscious wisdom of the individual.[5]

Jung also felt that dreams were a way to delve into the collective unconscious. To test his theory that there was a collective unconscious common to all cultures and societies, he used mythology. Traveling to Africa and to the United States, he studied African blacks and Native Americans. In his studies, he became convinced that there were two layers of consciousness: the *collective unconscious* and the *personal unconscious*. He believed that the collective unconscious contained archetypal symbols that represented the wisdom of all humanity. He called these primordial images "ancestral memory archetypes" and felt that the individual inherits these just as he or she inherits physical characteristics. To Jung, our personal unconscious was recognizable material from our past that had been forgotten or repressed.[6]

Jung noted that archetypal images appeared in the dreams of people who were in life-threatening or life-transforming situations. He observed that these images would appear when a person was experiencing illness, undergoing specific types of stress, or releasing an attitude or belief system. When a new orientation was needed, it was as if the person was connected with life force energy in the form of symbols. Jung felt that the archetype was a primordial image that met a need of the moment. He stated that true archetypal symbols were never invented. Someone could not consciously sit down and create a symbol. The symbols were already in the collective unconscious of all people.[7]

Jung liked to work with a series of dreams, associating one with the next and so on to unravel his patients' difficulties. Freud, however, concentrated on one dream at a time, viewing them as isolated incidents. Both had success with their patients, and their theories were appropriate for the time.[8]

ALFRED ADLER

Another associate of Freud, Alfred Adler, also disagreed with his techniques. Adler felt that the major influence on a person's character development was the struggle for power. He introduced into our language such terms as *sibling rivalry*, *inferiority complex*, and *superiority complex*. He felt that people were looking for meaning in life and that values and purposes were as necessary for life as were sex and power drives. Adler (1870–1937) did not focus on the concepts of the unconscious as Jung and Freud had. He saw dreams more in terms of wishful thinking and wish fulfillment. Unlike Freud, he did not see sex as an underlying cause. He felt that dreams were influenced by our urge for power.[9]

ERICH FROMM

Psychoanalyst Erich Fromm said that there was one universal language from which all languages developed. This was the symbolic language that appeared in dreams.[10]

Fromm divided symbols in dreams into three categories: conventional symbols, accidental symbols, and universal symbols. He believed that conventional symbols were symbols with only one actual meaning, like a stop sign or a plus sign or minus sign. Accidental symbols were symbols personal to the individual in the dream, or personal to a group of people, but not real to people in general. Universal symbols were those found to be common throughout the world, such as water representing emotion and intuition, and fire representing energy, power, purification, and transformation.[11]

3.

WHAT METAPHYSICIANS
SAY ABOUT DREAMS

Standing at the tip of the long, rocky jetty that extended far into the tranquil sea, I experienced a deep sense of contentment. Low-lying, opalescent clouds hugged the horizon, merging the cobalt-blue sky with the serene azure Hawaiian sea.

Without warning, an immense surge of water and foam roared up from the sea and a huge wave cascaded over the jetty. I desperately tried to cling to the jagged rocks, but I was ripped from my hold and thrown into the churning sea. Every ounce of strength was draining from me as I struggled to stay afloat. A powerful riptide sucked at my waterlogged clothes. I felt searing pain in my lungs as I inhaled salt water. I was drawn down into the dark, forbidding sea. . . .

Sweating and trembling uncontrollably, I sat up in bed and fumbled for the light—any light.

I let out a long sigh of relief. It was only a dream—I nestled into the cool comfort of my sheets, images slowly fading from my consciousness as I returned to a deep sleep. The morning disclosed no hint of the night's terror. In fact, I had no conscious memory of the dream.

As I was waking, a phone call interrupted the stillness of the morning. It was an invitation to go to the beach. It was such a clear, perfect day. My friend and I drove to an unfamiliar beach. There was a long jetty stretching into the sea. As we scrambled in exploration along the rocks, not even the smallest hint of the night's terror came to mind. I perched at the end of the jetty, gazing at the horizon where a lazy cloud melded the crystal sea and sky into one endless universe of blue. Then, suddenly, my mind was flooded with memories of the night before. With a desperate sense of urgency, I grabbed my friend and we quickly made our way back over the rocks. Puzzled, yet compliant, she scrambled to the security of the beach. From the shore we watched in disbelief as the sea began to churn, sending a powerful wave crashing over the jetty where we had stood only moments before.

I credit that dream for saving my life. I had had no knowledge that I was going to the beach, had never been to that particular beach, and had never seen any pictures of it. In the realm of science, my dream would probably be considered a coincidence. A scientist might rationalize that given the vast number of dreams an individual has, statistically there is a chance that one would come true at some point. The metaphysician, however, would consider this a dream of true prophecy.

In times long past, dreamers attributed their nightly visions to external forces. They believed that God, angels, nature spirits, gods and goddesses, various entities, and the spirits of their ancestors would visit them in the night hours, presenting themselves through dreams. Ancient dreamers deliberately invoked these influences by incubating their dreams (a process by which you select a dream topic and then program yourself for it). Spiritual truths and enlightenment gleaned during the dream state were used for telepathic purposes, prophecy, and other forms of ESP, as well as astral travel and communication with the dead.

Metaphysicians believe that dreams are not only neurons firing in the brain, as scientists believe, or psychological release of unresolved daytime difficulties, but that dreams are a way to touch the inner realms. The popularity of Carlos Castaneda's books regarding the Mexican mystic Don Juan exemplifies the interest in this belief system. Don Juan stated that dreams were aids to the development of psychic and mental powers. To increase these abilities, he affirmed that a person need only remain conscious while dreaming, learning how to control the dream itself. Maintaining consciousness during the dream state has been referred to as "lucid dreaming." (See chapter 9.)

Edgar Cayce, aptly referred to as the Sleeping Prophet, has often been considered the grandfather of metaphysical and psychic interpretation of dreams. The waking Edgar Cayce was known as a gifted professional photographer and admired as an amicable Sunday-school teacher. The sleeping Edgar Cayce, however, possessed a far broader and more colorful reputation. He was a gifted psychic, able to give valuable information that had a profound effect on thousands of people.[1]

The sleeping Edgar Cayce was a medical diagnostician and a visionary. The fascination with his life and work was reflected in 1954, when the University of Chicago awarded a Ph.D. based on a study of his work. In the thesis, Cayce was referred to as a religious seer.[2]

When Cayce was a young boy, he would fall asleep with his head resting on his school books; the following morning, he had absorbed information he had never consciously studied. As a result, Cayce was able to advance rapidly in school. This gift faded, however, and Cayce completed only seven grades.

When Cayce reached the age of twenty-one, he developed a gradual paralysis of the throat muscles which threatened the loss of his voice. Though several doctors were consulted, none was successful in discovering the cause of Cayce's condition. As a last resort, he asked a friend to assist him in moving into the same level of sleep that had enabled him to memorize his school books as a child. His friend gave him the appropriate suggestion, and at once Cayce entered a sleeplike state. (See chapter 10.) From this level of consciousness, he recommended medication and manipulative therapy for his own condition, and it healed the paralysis and restored his voice.[3]

As news traveled of Cayce's gift, many doctors in Kentucky began to use Cayce's unique talent to diagnose their patients. They learned that Cayce needed only the name and address of a patient in order to disclose, in a dream state, valuable information regarding that individual. By the time Edgar Cayce died in 1945, in Virginia Beach, Virginia, he had given thousands of people information over a period of forty-three years. One in twenty of his readings refers to dreams. Cayce regarded dreams as a kind of problem-solving exercise. He referred to dream incubation (see chapter 8) as a way to present solutions to daytime problems.[4]

Cayce continually illustrated how various dream symbols attempt to develop awareness within the dreamer. He felt that symbols could signify that it is time to develop new beliefs, to take more responsibility for life, to be more accepting, or to expand horizons. Cayce explained that all dreams were not necessarily problem solving in nature but often assisted in the self-transformation process of the dreamer. He advocated that certain series of dreams were devoted to developing new qualities within the dreamer, such as humility, nonjudgment, self-acceptance, love, and courage.[5]

Edgar Cayce believed that some dreams represented a new energy or change in a person's life and that certain dreams could even prophesy the future. For example, one woman wrote to Cayce relating a dream in which she saw five chrysanthemums resting on the grave of her husband's father. Cayce responded that within five weeks, her husband would have an experience of being taught by his deceased father through the medium of dreams. Cayce affirmed that the experience would be a joyful one. Within five weeks, the dreams did, in fact, come to her husband. Perhaps Cayce's greatest gift was his intuition with regard to health and dreams. He believed that people could not only receive signals of impending physical imbalances while in the dream state but also receive the cures within dreams.[6]

When a woman sorrowfully said that she had dreamed she would never be able to conceive a child, Cayce reassured her that she most definitely *would* give birth. He advised her to release any literal interpretation of the dream and counseled that the dream was simply encouraging her to take careful preparation for motherhood, especially with regard to her diet and her belief patterns. These were areas in which she required a rebirth within herself in order to conceive the child she so desperately wanted. Shortly thereafter, she became the joyful mother of a healthy baby.[7]

Cayce consistently urged his clients to solve their problems through their own interpretation of their dreams. Edgar Cayce's work made such an impact that it remains the foundation of a great portion of modern metaphysics.

Another aspect of dreams and metaphysics is the realm of reincarnation and karma. Reincarnation affirms that our true essence is spirit, not a mere body. As spirit, we incarnate repeatedly in various bodies in order to learn and grow. The central concept of karma is that whatever you sow, you reap. This law of cause and effect governs your experience over collective lifetimes. You balance karma during your waking hours, and you can also work through and culminate karmic lessons through your dreams. (See chapter 12.) There have been many reports of dreams in which someone who has died is reassuring the dreamer that the deceased is alive and well and that there is no further need to grieve. Occasionally, the deceased will instruct the dreamer in some basic concern of daily life. Let me share a powerful example of this from my experience.

I was working on Union Street in San Francisco at a healing center during a very rewarding time in my life. My shiatsu (pressure-point therapy similar to acupressure) practice was at a peak. My Zen training, with its disciplined commitment to focus, enhanced my ability to achieve a tremendous sense of clarity and healing with each point I pushed.

One evening as the San Francisco fog was settling in and I listened to foghorns sounding in the background, the phone rang. The call was from a friend who said hesitantly, with a voice full of emotion, "David's dead." David was a healer and a medical doctor who also worked at the center. He had a youthful exuberance and passion for life that permeated the entire clinic. My first thought was one of disbelief: Not David! He had had so much to live for. His practice was thriving, he and his wife had just purchased a beautiful home in Mill Valley, and they were joyfully anticipating the birth of a child. Why David?

That night in my dreams, a beckoning presence seemed to flutter at the edges of my consciousness. As I stumbled through the next few days feeling numb, I began to experience strange phenomena. When walking through various rooms in our Marina apartment, the lights would flicker on and off. Vaguely, I thought about calling an electrician. My dreams were filled with an elusive sense of urgency. I did not, however, connect any of this with David. I merely assumed it was part of my grieving process.

Just before Christmas, my shiatsu group gathered in my living room for a class. Our valiant little Christmas tree was radiant with miniature lights. As the class began, the non-blinking lights on the Christmas tree began to blink on and off. I explained to the group that we had been having trouble with our electrical system and that we should ignore it.

However, the lights continued to blink in a definite, steady sequence. Turning our attention back to the tree, an individual in the class asked it, "Are you trying to tell us something?" The tree lights responded with a pattern of blinks. It finally dawned on me that David had been attempting to make contact with me through my dreams in order to provide comfort and information to his grieving wife. With unfailing determination, he was now trying to contact me through our electrical system. We continued to ask yes and no questions, which he initially responded with the blinking lights, blinking once for yes and twice for no. Eventually we were able to garner information that he wished us to pass on to his wife. As soon as I gave his wife the necessary information, the dreams ceased and our electrical system returned to normal.

A psychologist would probably analyze my dreams during this time as a way to process and release my grief. The metaphysician, however, would perceive that David was indeed attempting to communicate with me in order to give me information. For me, the metaphysical interpretation is validated by the occurrence of the blinking lights and by the fact that the information to be relayed to his wife was valuable to her. Communication with deceased friends or family members is a skill that can be learned through dream incubation. (See chapter 8.)

The flying dream is another type of metaphysical dreaming. A psychologist would identify dream flying as a psychological sense of freedom expressed by the symbol of flying. To a metaphysician, however, dream flying is astral projection. Simply defined, astral projection occurs when one's soul literally leaves the body, connected only by a single cord of energy called an "astral cord," to explore other realms and dimensions. (See chapter 13.)

Another common metaphysical belief is that while we are dreaming, guides come to give us valuable information and insight. A guide is generally a discarnate being with whom you were connected in a previous lifetime. This being continues to be interested in you, working with you to provide guidance that benefits the evolution of your soul. When the conscious mind shuts down during sleep, guides have easier access to your inner self. (See chapter 17.)

DREAM WEAVERS

Ancestors, you have crossed over,
epic journey of the night,
to weave the fabric of our dreams
reflections of our innermost realms.

Deft masters of the dream loom
ever mindful of the texture and dye
of one thread against another,
we follow the footsteps of your
crossing.

—M. Anne Sweet

4.
ANCIENT DREAMERS

And it shall come to pass afterward that I shall pour out my spirit on all flesh; your sons and your daughters shall prophesy, your old men shall dream dreams and your young men shall see visions. —Joel 2:28

Somewhere in the window of your memory, elusive moments hover just out of your conscious reach. You may sense them waiting there, yet when you reach out to touch them, you find they quickly slip away. These moments are beyond the world of form and illusion. They dwell in the mysterious realm of dreams.

Throughout history, in every culture, there have been rare individuals who have stepped through the sleepers' veil to listen to messages of the night. These dream weavers have carried back with them precious gifts through that dim portal into wakeful reality. They have brought delicate weblike dreams from the silent spaces to lead the destiny of men and nations alike.

Though the histories of most of the countless nocturnal mystics have been lost forever, a few tales have survived. One such story concerns an emperor of the Shang Dynasty, Wu Ting (1324–1266 B.C.). When one of his most trusted counselors died, Wu Ting was devastated by the loss. He presented ritual offerings to the Ruler of the Gods, Shang-Ti, and asked this god to show him who should be the successor to his beloved counselor. He then had a dream in which he clearly saw the face of the new counselor. This dream was so vivid that he was able to have a portrait made of the dream man's face. Unable to find this person, he had the painting taken throughout the empire. Only one man was found whose face matched the portrait, and he was only a common worker. Yet Wu Ting's faith in his dream was so complete that he elevated this man to the position of prime minister of his empire.[1]

Researchers believe that three hundred to four hundred temples were erected in ancient Greece for the purpose of practicing dream control. These temples, thought to be in existence for more than a thousand years, were used as facilities for physical and emotional healing.[2] Within these temples, help was evoked from the gods. Hypnos, the god of sleep, was said to fan mortals with his wings to induce slumber. Then Zeus would give Morpheus, the god of dreams, warnings, prophecies, and inspirations to send to humanity via the winged messenger, Hermes.[3]

The seeking of special dreams to invoke the powers of the gods is called dream incubation. (See chapter 8.) In ancient Greece, incubation occurred when a person slept in a sacred place after going through a ritual of purification. The purification usually involved abstinence from alcohol, meat, and sexual relations, along with an offering made to a selected deity.[4]

Many of the sacred Greek shrines such as Delphi, the Shrine of Apollo, and the Temple of Epidaurus were dream oracles, or places where the deities were thought to reveal the secrets of inner knowledge. It was to these shrines that the sick would journey, hoping that Asclepius, the god of medicine and healing, would appear to them in their sleep. It is recorded that Asclepius offered advice in the form of herbal remedies and, on occasion, awarded instantaneous cures. He was thought to appear to his patients in their dreams, mixing potions and applying bandages to the sufferers' bodies and in some instances summoning sacred snakes to lick the ailing areas. Those desiring a cure would sleep among non-poisonous snakes, as snakes were thought to be the symbolic carriers of healing. The association has carried forward in the modern caduceus, the symbol of two intertwined snakes signifying healing.[5]

It is interesting to note that in the yoga tradition, a coiled snake represents the kundalini life force embodied in the base of the spine. The kundalini energy is believed to be the potency of the universe manifest within the human being.

Hippocrates, the ancient Greek physician and father of modern medicine, once said, "Some dreams are divinely inspired and others are the direct result of the physical body." He believed that the appearance of the sun, moon, stars, and natural phenomena were significant to the understanding of a person's health and well-being. If the sky in a dream was very clear, then the person's body was thought to be functioning normally. If the stars, for example, were not clear or were falling from the sky, this signified a disturbance in the person's health. Hippocrates stated in his treatise on dreams, "It is a sign of sickness if the dream star appears dim or moves either westward or down into the earth or sea, or upward. Upward movement indicates fluxes [unusual discharges] in the head. Movement into the sea, disease of the bowels. Eastward movement, growing of tumours in the flesh."[6]

These symbolic interpretations might not be appropriate today, but they show the respect given to dream symbols in ancient times. It was noted in those ancient days that prior to the onset of disease, a dream would occur with the symptoms of that illness. In fact, these dreams today are called "prodromic," which is derived from the Greek word *prodromos*, meaning "running before."[7]

Galen, the second-century Greek physician, and Aristotle, founder of the science of logic, believed that dreams reflected the bodily state and could therefore be used to diagnose and treat illness. Plato considered the liver the seat of dreams, and in his famous work *Timeaeus* he claimed that prophetic dreams were received through the liver. Pliny held that dreams were supernatural in origin. In ancient Greece, dream interpreters were in great demand, much the same as medical doctors are today. Among the items looked for by dream interpreters were dream gates. In ancient Grecian dreams, two dream gates would appear, one consisting of ivory and the other of horn. If the dreamer saw the ivory gate, it was interpreted as a warning. If he or she saw the horn gate, the meaning was deemed prophetic.[8]

Several ancient civilizations revered dreams. In fact, four of the oldest civilizations—China, India, the Middle East, and Egypt—have left records indicating their use of dreams.

Dream incubation was widely practiced in Egypt from 4000 B.C. to 2000 B.C. The Egyptian pharaohs held dreams in great esteem, believing they were vehicles of guidance from the gods. Between the paws of the Great Sphinx is a slab of pink granite inscribed with the dream of a man who became an Egyptian king. One day while he was sleeping in the shade of the Sphinx, Ra, the sun god, appeared to him and told him that he would one day become the ruler of all Egypt. When he woke, he noticed that the Sphinx was covered with sand and in need of repair. He made a commitment that if he ever became ruler, the Sphinx would always be kept in perfect condition. A few years later, true to the dream, he became Thothmes IV. Loyal to his promise, the ruler restored the Sphinx, and it has been maintained ever since.[9]

In Egypt, Imhotep was the equivalent of the Greek god Asclepius. In the Shrine of Asclepius-Imhotep in Egypt reside records of the interpretations of various dreams. One is inscribed, "A bed on fire means your partner is unfaithful to you."[10]

In ancient Syria, this was a special prayer for dreams:

> *My gracious god, stand by me.*
> *My friendly god will listen to me.*
> *God Mamu of my dreams,*
> *My god, send me a favourable dream.*[11]

In the Middle East, the practice of *istigara* was used to receive a dream that would answer a question. The *istigara* was a special dream prayer said just before falling asleep.[12]

Even the Old and New Testaments mention that God's will would be made known through the dreams and visions of the prophets. In fact, there are some twenty well-documented accounts that refer to divine guidance being given through dreams. In some cases, these dreams changed the course of destiny. Moses was instructed by God to listen for Him in his dreams. "Hear now my words. If there be a prophet among you, I, the Lord, will make myself known to him in a vision and will speak to him in a dream."[13]

In another account, an angel appeared to Joseph in a dream and said, "Joseph, thou son of David, fear not to take unto thee Mary, thy wife, for that which is conceived in her is of the Holy Ghost."[14]

In ancient Japan, dream incubation was practiced in both the Buddhist and the Shinto temples. Several Buddhist temples were famous as dream oracles. The procedure for obtaining a visionary dream was as follows. First, there was a period of abstinence, and a journey was made to the holy site where an offering was given. The dreamer would remain for a specified time of either seven, twenty-one, or one hundred days. These numbers were considered significant. The dreamer would sleep adjacent to the inner sanctum awaiting a special dream. It was believed that divinity dwelled in the inner sanctum. Often a healing dream would be requested (much as it would be in ancient Greece), and the Bodhisattva Kannon would appear in the dreams, healing ailments.[15]

Regardless of which culture practiced dream healing, it was always the reigning deity who would come forth to effect the cure. In order to penetrate the same inner spaces touched by these ancient dreamers, see chapter 8. This will help you to create your personal dream temple and to incubate dreams as was done in ancient times.

5.
NATIVE DREAMERS

In the mist of dawn, the shaman dances,
head bowed in the ritual of his forefathers,
chanting rhythmic incantations,
solemn invocations to the spirit of the lake.
— M. Anne Sweet

*T*he evening embers are dying. The lone cry of a solitary owl pierces the cold stillness. In the shadows, tribal members silently return to their tepees. The time of the big hunt is approaching, and tonight is set aside for dreaming. Tribal members embrace the quiet comfort of awaiting night guardians. These dream guides are called upon to lend assistance and guidance during the night. Tonight, their advice is sought as to where and when to hunt. Starry diamonds sprinkle the black sky. A shooting star punctuates the silence.

In the morning there is a gathering, and each dream is shared—and with each dream, certainty of the location and strategy of the hunt becomes clearer. The tribe knows that their survival depends on these dreams.

A Native American Proverb:
Respect your brother's dreams.

Native Americans gave special meaning to dreams. Dreams were used by almost every tribe to predict the future, manage psychological problems, heal sexual difficulties, and cure ailments. Each tribe had very specific techniques for obtaining and understanding dreams. The study of the use of dreams among Native American cultures is a very complex one. This chapter touches only briefly on their use of dreams.[1]

To the Native Americans, there existed only a thin line between the dream and wakeful states. They believed Mother Earth was a real entity and a powerful source of strength, and that the Creator pervaded all things in nature. They believed it was during the evening hours that one could access the Creator, ancestors, and inner guidance. As a result, Indians gave great power to dreams.

In the Mohawk villages, it was common for dreamers to become so inspired by images in their dreams that they would create poems or riddles. They would then give or receive gifts based on whether or not other members of the tribe could answer the riddle.[2]

The Seneca tribe worked very intimately with their dreams. They demanded that each dream be acted out either symbolically or literally. It was this aspect of their culture that made their conversion to Christianity by the early French Jesuit missionaries extremely difficult.[3]

Each of the tribes of the Iroquois nation—Mohawk, Oneida, Onondaga, Cayuga, Seneca, and Huron—called the Six Nations, participated in its unique daily dream ritual. They would gather each year for a special joint ritual sometime after the first snowfall. These determined Indians traveled great distances to attend the gatherings. When they arrived, they would each act out their dreams wearing masks. Occasionally, they would wear costumes along with the masks. At other times, they would perform naked except for a mask. The yearly festival of this traveling dream theater was known as the *Onoharoia*; it allowed many *Ondinnonk* to be acted out very dramatically. Many of the ritual masks of the Iroquois tribes were used in these ceremonies. Young men would perform in these dream shows, traveling from Indian settlement to settlement to act out their dreams.[4]

The people of the Iroquois tribes believed so strongly in the importance of *Ondinnonk* that they felt a person would become sick and even die if his dreams were not acted out.[5]

The ancient Aborigines of Australia believed in the power of dreams. Their rich and profound dream world encompassed much more than the dreams at night and still remains a mystery to the Western world. However, nighttime dreams were considered very important and daily activities were often regulated by the sharing of dreams and their interpretations. Some Aboriginal tribes believed that everything was a dream before the coming of white men.

Dream Guides

Central to most native tribes was the concept of a guardian or guide whom one could access while awake as well as during a dream. A psychologist might rationalize this as a gestalt conversation with an imaginary being who, in truth, is really an unacknowledged aspect of oneself. However, to the native people, the guide was very real. Their dream friends were as real as the friends whom they could touch during waking hours. Frequently, they would fast in order to gain a dream guide, a special dream, or a dream song (a song presenting itself during sleep). Dreamers would sometimes compose dream songs without fasting. However, lack of food may, in some unknown way, enhance this mysterious creative process. Perhaps the thin air unique to the high mountains and rocky places preferred by some Native Americans as places to fast also influenced the quality of their dreams.

Research indicates that when an individual is involved in

extremely quiet pursuits, he is more apt to experience a greater number of dreams than when busy with social activities. He will also have longer REM cycles each night—as much as 60 percent more REM sleep. Increased isolation seems to cause an increase in dreaming. Total isolation can produce hallucinations in some people. Physical inactivity is also a factor in causing increased dreaming.[6]

Native American Use of Dreams

Native Americans had a variety of practical uses for their dreams. In addition to discovering times and places for hunting and planting, they also used dreams to determine names. They would incubate or ask for the name of a new child, and the name would come in a dream. (See chapter 8.) Frequently, creative dances and songs came during dreams. Numerous cultural artifacts are believed to have had their origins in dreams. Some of the decorative patterns on blankets, paintings, jewelry, and clothing are also thought to have been conceived during dreams.

Common Traits of Native Cultures

The following traits are evident in all native cultures that possess a high regard for dreams.

- Dreams are considered vital to success in life. This attitude made it easier to recall and interpret dreams for the ancient people and remains true today.
- Supernatural figures appear in dreams granting special powers or giving important information.
- Shamans (medicine women and men) are expected to use their dreams to acquire knowledge.
- Dreams are induced by utilizing techniques such as sleeping alone in a power spot or a sacred place, or by fasting.[7]

Interestingly, research indicates that 80 percent of all hunting and fishing societies use dreams to seek and control supernatural powers, while only 20 percent of all agricultural and animal-raising societies use dreams for this purpose. Thus, it appears that the more dependent a tribe was on hunting and fishing, the more likely it would be to use dreams.[8]

To some extent, dreams are now relics of the human mind. However, in the recent past, native people had a direct path to their dreams. They knew that as they lived close to nature and moved in harmony with all cycles of nature, it was far easier to access the mystical world of dreams. They were able to directly access the meanings and images of their dreams. Now, as our societies have moved farther and farther away from nature, we have forgotten our ability to access our dreams directly and easily.

We can glean wisdom from the ancient Native Americans. Take off a day or a week and spend time in nature, away from electricity and machines. Rely on your resources. Get back in touch with the cycles of nature. Spend time in the moonlight, allowing it to bathe you. As a result of this gentle respite, you will find it much easier to access your dreams.

DREAM MAKERS

*In the beginning, the attempt of our crossing
is clumsy, unsteady, the way is
mysterious and unclear, our dreams
are woven of thick coarse wool.*

*Along the way, we find the vestiges
of our ancestors, ancient dream weavers,
left as guideposts, illuminators, lighting
our way, refining the quality of our weave.*

—M. Anne Sweet

6.

DREAM RECALL

*The reason we can't see around
the corner is so we don't miss
the beauty here and now.*
   —Karl Bettinger

Your dreams can provide you with fantasy, adventure, and romance. They can serve as a mystical key to foretell the future and unravel the past. Your dreams can rival Hollywood in providing you with entertainment, but with *you* as producer, director, and star— all worthy of Oscars. However, if you want to recall your dreams, you need to remain cognizant and alert at all times or you will forget the roles you have played. You also will forget the other actors and the significance of each one. You will undoubtedly forget the lines you spoke even before awakening. Just as it requires skill for an actor to memorize his lines, it requires skill for a dreamer to recall his dreams.

The single most important element in remembering dreams is motivation. To acquire that motivation, you must first perceive your dreams as worthwhile; regard them as valuable messages received from your subconscious. It is imperative that you believe they deserve to be heard.

Contemplate each dream as if it were a brilliant gem with each lustrous facet reflecting a clean and remarkable new insight into yourself. View each dream as if it were allowing you to gaze deeply from a rich new perspective into the shimmering jewel called you. From these different perspectives, you will gain great wisdom in understanding yourself. Therefore, if you regard your dreams as valuable and useful, you will be motivated to recall them.

Dream Recall Blockages

If you are unable to remember your dreams at present, perhaps some attitude is blocking your ability to do so. To see whether you have such an attitude, participate in the simple process outlined on the following pages. This will help you to become aware of and release limitations, even those hidden in your subconscious, that are blocking your dream recall.

During this process, you will be given a list of some of the more common attitudes that make dream recall difficult. One or more of the beliefs might apply to you. Take time to read the list thoughtfully *out loud*. If any of the statements seems to fit or feels right, be ready to jot down your experience.

On a separate sheet of paper, note the following headings, leaving room for a sentence or two after each.

ATTITUDE

Thought response:

Emotional response:

> *Body response:*
>
>
> *Affirmation:*

YOUR THOUGHT RESPONSE

If you have read a specific statement (attitude) that seems true for you, notice the *thoughts* you are having in response to that statement. Observe what you are thinking in terms of any denial or affirmation. Note whatever thoughts occur to you as a result of hearing yourself say this attitude out loud. Above all, remain honest with yourself. Keep in mind that there is no right or wrong thought. This exercise is simply to assist you in recalling your dreams.

YOUR EMOTIONAL RESPONSE

Observe your emotional response to hearing or reading the statement. What specific emotions does the attitude in question generate in you? Remember, do not judge your response, simply notice it. *The very act of examining attitudes will allow you to release them.*

YOUR BODY RESPONSE

Notice your body's response. Even when it seems difficult to be conscious of thought or emotional responses, your body will often send its own clear messages. It *is* responding, though subtly at times, to the attitudes spoken, and it is possible for you to become aware of these responses. As you state the attitude, practice learning to recognize even those slight changes within your body. It might only be a small tightening in the center of your chest or a twitch in your left eye. Your body is always giving you clues. Listen to it. It can be used as a valuable indicator of concerns still blocking your dream recall.

YOUR AFFIRMATION

The last section on your list, Affirmation, is something you create for yourself. An affirmation is a positive thought that reaffirms the direction in which you want your thoughts to go. Find or create an affirmation that will release the attitude that is blocking your ability to recall your dreams. Attitudes form pathways that thoughts travel. They are well-worn pathways you consistently choose, without thinking, as you would cross a field of tall grasses. If a person has the attitude "Dreams are of no consequence," every time the word *dream* comes to mind, it is as if the mind runs down the path labeled, "Dreams are of no importance." This path can become so worn that it requires conscious effort to create a new path.

Likewise, a positive thought or affirmation, "My dreams are valuable and important," will begin to create a new pathway. Eventually, if affirmed often enough, the new pathway will replace the old. When a thought regarding dreams occurs, the mind will begin to travel the new path and reinforce the thought that dreams are valuable. As a result, it becomes easier to recall dreams.

At the end of this section are some suggested affirmations to enhance dream recall.

Attitudes That Block Dream Recall

Say these out loud and note your internal response.

I don't feel that dreams are important.

I'm not sure I really want to know what's in my subconscious.

I need sleep. Dreams prevent me from getting a good night's sleep.

I might learn things about the future that I don't want to know.

Maybe we're not meant to remember.

Sexuality in dreams is disturbing.

I might have nightmares.

I feel out of control in my dreams and that's uncomfortable for me.

I might open myself up to psychic forces.

It's distressing to do things in my dreams that are inconsistent with my waking values.

Something difficult happened in my past and I don't want to think about it or dream about it.

It takes too much time and effort to remember dreams.

These are only a few of the attitudes held by people who don't recall their dreams. As you check to see if any of these are appropriate for you, see if there are other attitudes as well that apply to you. Remember, just becoming aware of and exploring attitudes often is enough to cause them to dissipate so that dreams can be recalled more easily.

Following is an example of how your experience might appear on your chart.

ATTITUDE

I don't feel that dreams are important.

Thought response:
I feel that they are important to *other* people who are having problems.

Emotional response:
When I say this attitude, I feel some irritation and even anger.

Body response:
After saying this attitude, I notice that I am not breathing very fully and my lower neck muscles feel tight.

Affirmation:
There is *great* importance in dreams. My dreams allow me to unlock unseen potential within myself. I enjoy dreaming and I remember my dreams easily.

Affirmations That Promote Dream Recall

I enjoy dreaming and I remember my dreams easily.

My emotions are valuable and I appreciate my emotional dream life.

I have all the time I need to remember dreams and to assimilate them.

I accept my past unconditionally and know that everything that has ever happened to me in my life and my dreams was necessary for me to get where I am now.

My dreams give me valuable perceptions that allow for more balance and joy in my life.

Dreaming allows me to be more creative and I love recalling my dreams.

I do not judge my dreams. I know that every message from my subconscious deserves to be heard.

Dreaming gives me valuable information about the future.

I deserve sexual pleasure and it's enjoyable to experience dream sex.

I give myself permission to recall and understand the deeper meaning of my dreams.

There is *great* importance to dreams. My dreams allow me to unlock unseen potential within myself. I enjoy dreaming and I remember my dreams easily. So be it!

Diary of Dreams . . . Your Dream Journal

I never travel without my diary. One should always have something sensational to read in the train.

—Oscar Wilde

A dream journal is a record of your inner journeys, your inner quest for self-understanding. Recording just one or two dreams, however, will not provide you with nearly enough information. Carl Jung felt that true self-knowing came from observing and interpreting a series of dreams over a long period of time, perhaps even years. He felt that in this way a person could begin to weave a tapestry of the recurring themes pervading his or her life. As you continue your daily dream journal, you will gain an understanding of your destiny. Your diary of dreams can literally become your personal book of wisdom.

Dreams are forgotten very easily (usually within ten minutes of awakening), and it takes an enormous amount of willpower to pull them back into conscious thought.

Research has revealed that dreaming is accompanied by rapid eye movement (REM). Sleepers awakened during REM sleep were in the middle of a dream. Sleepers awakened during bodily movement immediately following REM sleep recounted completed dreams. Five minutes after REM sleep, the sleepers remembered only fragments of dreams. Ten minutes after REM sleep, the sleepers had virtually no recall. Thus, it is literally within the first few seconds of awakening that a dream is still vivid. Consequently, it is imperative that you write down your dream as soon as you wake, while it remains fresh in your memory. Write down as many details as you can recall.

(Lucid dreams, however, because you are a conscious partici-
pant, will remain in the memory for a much longer time. See
chapter 9.)

What You Will Need to Record Your Dreams

1. An easy-flowing pen
2. A notebook, journal, or tape recorder (preferably a Dictaphone)
3. Flashlight or night light (if using a notebook)
4. Easily seen clock

EASY-FLOWING PEN

Be sure you have a pen that writes easily without pressure,
such as a felt-tip pen. Do not use pencil, as it writes too lightly
for notes taken when you are very sleepy. Place both pen and
diary next to your bed.

If you prefer pens that have their own lights, these can be
bought at medical supply shops. A less costly way to accomplish this is to purchase a penlight and tape it to your pen.

NOTEBOOK OR JOURNAL

The best kind of dream journal is a spiral-bound notebook. A
loose-leaf notebook is not as useful, as the papers can slide and
move while you write.

Divide your notebook into two sections. On the left side,
you will write the date, hour, and all the details of your
dream. On the right side, you will note your interpretation.
(See pages 60–61.)

It is important to write the date in your journal ahead of
time, as this sets up a positive expectancy that you will record
your dream on that date. Recording the date can also make
it easy for you to notice and record a realization later

concerning a particular dream on a specific date. For example, you may have had a powerful dream on October 24 and then later realized that was your mother's birthday. While not being consciously aware of it at the time, your mind was responding to your emotions and feelings toward your mother. Later, having this information may provide you with valuable insights regarding you and your relationship with your mother.

You might also want to jot down in your journal the heading, Dream One. This again sets up a positive expectancy that you will have more than one dream during the night. As soon as you have recorded your first dream of the evening, and before you go back to sleep, write Dream Two in your journal, setting up the expectancy of a second dream.

When recording your dream, also note the feelings you experienced in the dream. Jot down predominant colors, symbols, key words, themes, and emotions. Try not to get so stuck on a detail that you forget the rest of the dream. If you heard a poem or an interesting expression or phrase, record that information first. Then record the visual parts you remember, as they tend to be retained longer than anything heard in a dream.

For individuals who find it difficult to wake up enough to turn on a flashlight or a tape recorder, there is an eyes–closed technique. As you awaken, feel for the notebook next to your bed. Then, with your eyes still closed so that you remain involved in your dream, begin to write. You will have to experiment to find a way to avoid writing over what you have already written. One method is to extend the little finger of your writing hand as a guide in finding the top or side edge of the paper; this gives you some indication of where you are. Some people who have difficulty reading their nighttime writing prefer to scribble their dreams on scrap paper and later transfer it into their two-sided notebook.

HOW TO SET UP YOUR DREAM JOURNAL

DREAM 1

Date   *Here is where you write*
Time   *your interpretation of*
Location   *the dream.*

*Note everything
that you can
remember, every word
or image. Write the first
thing that comes into
your head even if it
doesn't seem like a
dream.*

*Note your feelings while
involved in the dream.*

*Record anything you
heard.*

*Note colors, symbols,
key words, themes, and
emotions.*

EXAMPLE OF A DREAM JOURNAL ENTRY

DREAM 1

Date: December 7
Time: 4:20 AM
Location: home

My car isn't working
properly. I look under
the hood and notice that
the radiator is empty. I
keep adding water and it
keeps coming out of a
hole in the bottom.

The feeling is one of
frustration.

INTERPRETATION
The radiator is the cooling
device of the car. If it's empty,
the car overheats. My car
seems to symbolize my body or
me. Also, to me water represents spirituality. I keep
emptying my spirituality out of
myself. If I keep doing this, I
will overheat and I won't be
able to run or function. I feel
that this dream is telling me to
spend some time being still and
attuning to my spiritual side. I
think it also means drink more
water. (I later found out that
my steering fluid had leaked out
during the night, giving the
dream a somewhat psychic
aspect as well.)

TAPE RECORDER

The advantage of using a tape recorder is that you can usually
stay more in touch with your vivid dream images than when
you write them down. For those who have a hard time falling
back to sleep after writing, a tape recorder is an excellent tool,
enabling you to record more detail in less time. One disadvantage to using a tape recorder is that you will later need to

transcribe the dream into your journal. Another disadvantage is that while it may seem that you are communicating clearly, in the morning you may not be able to understand your midnight ramblings. Very often your voice will sound as if you have come from another dimension, and, in fact, you have. If you use a tape recorder, you might consider getting the small hand-held type that is used for dictation. In the dark, these are easier to use than the larger models.

FLASHLIGHT
A battery-operated light is valuable if you are writing in your journal at night. Although small flashlights work well, the small battery-operated lanterns sold in camping-supply shops seem to work best. Using one of these will keep you from having to juggle the flashlight as you write.

EASILY SEEN CLOCK
It is valuable to note the time of your dreams so that you can begin to see patterns in your dreaming, especially if you are working with the ancient Chinese meridians (see chapter 23).

Begin to Record Your Dreams

- Put your tape recorder or journal next to your bed with your flashlight, pen, and clock.
- Lie in a position that allows your spine to be straight while you program yourself for dream recall.
- Choose one of the Before Sleep Techniques (see below).
- Sweet dreams!

Before-Sleep Dream Recall Techniques

TIBETAN DREAM MEDITATION

As you lie down to go to sleep, *concentrate on your desire for dream recall*. Now focus your attention on the back of your throat. Imagine a glowing blue sphere in the throat area and imagine putting your desire for dream recall within that blue orb. Hold that visualization until you fall asleep. Using this technique, you may find that your dream recall is greatly increased. It is interesting to note that this ancient Tibetan technique has an interesting physiological parallel. Research has shown that it is this area at the back of the throat (the stem of the brain) that controls the activation of dream states. Thus, it may be by connecting with this potent area before sleep, you begin the stimulation of dream activity and recall.

WATER TECHNIQUE

Drink half of a glass of water before retiring. As you drink, affirm to yourself, "Tonight I remember my dreams." When you wake in the morning, if no dream recall is evident, drink the remaining half of the glass of water, saying to yourself, "My dreams are recalled, now and through the day." Often drinking the second half of the glass of water stimulates dream recall. Sometimes that recall will occur spontaneously during the day.

THIRD EYE TECHNIQUE

This technique also uses water for dream recall. Put a bowl of water next to your bed. Right before sleep, dip two fingers into the water and lightly touch your throat. Then rub these two fingers on your forehead in the area of your third eye (the area between and slightly above your eyes). As you rub this area, affirm that you will remember your dreams. The next morning, again touch these areas with water. Very often this will stimulate recall.

SPIRITUAL ASSISTANCE

Relax your body, keeping your spine straight. Let your mind become still and receptive. Pray or ask your dream guide for assistance in remembering your dreams. (See chapter 5.) Strongly affirm that you will remember your dreams and repeat this to yourself several times as you fall asleep.

CREATIVE VISUALIZATION

As you begin to fall asleep, visualize yourself waking up, looking at the clock, noting the time, and writing down a dream. Continue this visualization forward in time until you see yourself waking in the morning and writing down another dream. Visualize yourself looking and feeling very satisfied because you have recorded your dreams.

FOUR DIRECTIONS TECHNIQUE

This technique has several parts and is an excellent method not only to remember but to obtain a vision dream.

1. When you enter the area where you will sleep, smudge the area with sage, cedar, juniper, or sweet grasses. Smudging means to offer or hold the smoldering herbs so that the smoke goes to each of the sacred directions—north, east, south, and west, and to Mother Earth and Father Sky (below and above). Smudge the area around your body for purification. This ancient ritual is for dedication and purification. It was felt that there could be direct communion with the Creator through smoke. One's prayers rise through the smoke, and the Creator sends messages or blessings down to the person through the smoke.

2. When you get into bed, replay each action of the day, moving backward to the time when you woke in the morning. Then begin the day anew in your mind, replaying each event from morning onward, changing your response to any situation in which you wish you had behaved differently. For instance, if you judged someone wrongly, review the situation—but this time, with understanding and kindness.

3. Say a prayer of thanks for the goodness in each day and affirm your intention to live a balanced and compassionate life.

4. Imagine an upward-spiraling double helix of energy spinning through you as you count backward from ten to one, affirming that you will remember your dreams. Your very last thoughts before sleep are very often the ones that affect your dreams.

5. Ask for the guidance of the Creator in your dreams. Ask for a revelation of the path you are to follow.

6. In the morning, give thanks for all that you have received.

After-Sleep Dream Recall Techniques

ROLLING TECHNIQUE
Research has shown that dreamers usually roll over or change positions immediately after a dream. It is thought that this helps you to move into a different brain-wave pattern. If you can't recall your dreams, change your position, sometimes this will spontaneously generate dream images. It seems that the dream is coded into the position that you were in while you had it, and gently rolling over can initiate recall.

CONVERSATION
Immediately after waking up, share with someone what you remember. Just beginning to talk about your dream will allow more of it to rise to your consciousness.

WRITING

When you write in your dream journal, just write whatever you remember, even if it's only a word or a feeling. If you don't remember anything, write, "I don't remember my dream." Very often this will stimulate dream recall. Or write down how you feel about not remembering, as this frequently gives a clue to the dream.

IMAGING

Imagine that it is the night before and you are getting ready for bed—brushing your teeth, lying down, and going to sleep. Then just watch the images and feelings that occur, even using your imagination. (Where do you think imagination comes from anyway?)

DOODLE TECHNIQUE

If you didn't remember your dream, begin to doodle in your dream journal. Often this triggers associations and sparks your memory.

COLOR TECHNIQUE

In this process, get a sense of what color your dream *felt* like and begin coloring or imagining that color to incite recall.

GESTALT

Put out two pillows. Sit on one and say to the other, "Okay, dreams, why aren't you coming into my memory?" Then move to the other pillow and answer, for example, "You are always in such a rush in the morning, I never feel that I have time to come forward." Move back and forth between the pillows as the dialogue continues. Notice the different voices and body positions you use for each of the two pillows. The conversation can be written as well as verbalized.

MOOD SAVORING

With your eyes still closed, notice your mood. Indulge in your mood. The mood that you are in when you awaken often reflects the activity in your dreams. Exaggerating your mood often stimulates dream memory.

Dream Recall Hints

Write it down. No matter how sure you are that you will remember the dream, you most probably will not. Write it down.

Don't move. When you write in your journal immediately after a dream, try to move as little as possible. Research in dream laboratories has shown that movement often impairs recall. When people roll over as they are awakened from a dream, they have a more difficult time remembering the dream. (Use the rolling technique only if there isn't *any* dream memory.)

Watch those flashes. Often, a dream doesn't appear but you have a vague feeling that one is just around the corner of your mind. It is as if it is delicately perched on the edge of your consciousness, waiting for some familiar element in your waking life to stimulate recall. These images can be so fleeting that you must remain conscious of the images that suddenly pop into your mind. Watch those images that flash into your mind during the day.

Beware the fragment trap. Even if it's only a dream fragment, record it. It can be important for self-understanding.

Record each dream as it occurs. It is difficult to record all your dreams every morning. Laboratory tests have shown that even if someone does remember all their dreams in the morning, they are less vivid and detailed than if they were recorded as they occurred. Just imagine watching four or five movies over an eight-hour period and then trying to remember them all at one time. Your memory is more exact if you record your dreams as they occur.

Sleep for shorter periods. Try to sleep two or three times a day. If you can change your sleeping patterns so that you have five hours of sleep at night and then one or two naps you will feel more refreshed because you are constantly refreshing yourself and you will recall your dreams much more easily.

Read and study. Learn as much as you can about dreams. Where intention goes, energy flows. As you increase your awareness in the area of dreams, you will increase your ability to recall your dreams.

Name that dream! When writing in your journal, give each of your dreams a descriptive title. These are good reference guides for later.

Wake up naturally. Train yourself to wake up before your alarm. Waking up to a jarring noise often alters the quality of your dream.

Hard case? If you still don't remember your dreams, you'll have to find a way to sleep more lightly. Drink a lot of water before bed so you'll have to get up during the night to go to the bathroom. Sleep in a chair. Any way that you can think of to sleep lightly contributes to your dream recall.

Even nightmares! Write down all your dreams, even nightmares and other dreams that you *don't* feel good about. We are not just "good." We are whole, a balance of light and dark, yin and yang, good and bad. We are total, infinite beings. It is important to honor and accept all aspects of ourselves. Every dream is important. As you write it down, affirm that this dream is indeed important.

Resist the urge! Resist trying to explain away the dream by relating it to a late-night snack, a television show that you saw right before bed, or a book that you were reading. These activities are just triggers for you to reach into a deeper part of your psyche. Fifty other people seeing that same TV show would have fifty different dreams. Similarly, if you are awakened by a dog barking and you dream that you are surrounded by raging wild dogs, someone else, under the same circumstances, might dream about his favorite childhood dog bounding toward him. Each dream can be explained by the barking, but each dream has important symbols that are unique to the dreamer.

Don't feel guilty if you forgot to remember a dream. Guilt will only hinder your progress. And if you do feel guilty, don't feel guilty about feeling guilty.

Meaning? You don't need to figure out the meaning of every dream. Often, just reviewing a dream several times will greatly contribute to your inner balance. Love and enjoy your dreams, interpreted or not!

Fun! It's not necessary to record all your dreams. If you don't feel like doing it, don't force yourself. Dream recall and recording should be fun!

7.
DREAM AIDS

The sun is shining warm flickers on the waves
I float above the beach, moving on a thought . . .
a sound draws me across the bridge . . .
I shut off the alarm!
Quick! Back across the bridge to . . . to . . .
    where?
I must have been dreaming . . .
                          —Karl Bettinger

*P*otions, totems, and nature's rhythms and cycles have been an integral part of the healing and visionary arts of shamans, kahunas, seers, magi, druids, and medicine men and medicine women. Throughout ancient lore and recorded history, there has always been reference to power objects used to facilitate divination and inner knowing. Today, you can use these tools for deeper exploration of your dream realm.

Stones

Ever since man first appeared on this planet, stones have been held in great esteem. The Aboriginal peoples of the world, as well as mystical secret societies, have passed on their unique uses of stones to assist in understanding the unseen realms.

The stones discussed here are but a few that can be used to assist dreaming. It's important to remember that of themselves these stones can do nothing. It is your *intention* that activates them for dream use.

MOONSTONE

The moonstone, with its silvery-white light undulating on its surface, is sacred in India. It is thought to bring good fortune. Used as a gift for lovers, it is believed to arouse tender passion and give lovers the ability to see into the future.

In many cultures it is felt that this stone changes with the phases of the moon. As the cycles of the moon are connected to dream cycles, the moonstone connects us more deeply with our inner dream states.

The moonstone is also soothing to the emotions. It can enhance physical and emotional balance for women during their menses. As the cycles of the moon are very connected to dream cycles, the moonstone connects us more deeply with our inner dream states. Sleep with a moonstone near you or tape a small one on your third eye area. As you fall asleep, dedicate your moonstone to your dream life by holding the intention that the moonstone will stimulate dreams.

SELENITE

This very translucent crystal is ruled by the moon. It is named after Selene, the Greek goddess of the moon. This very powerful stone is used to gain understanding of one's personal truth. It can allow for a deep calming and the attainment of profound inner states. It symbolizes pure spirit and can be used for spiritual advancement. Selenite is also an alchemic key to the past and the future.

Selenite is associated with your crown chakra and is a powerful tool for developing intuition and telepathic powers through your dreams. Use it for stimulating dreams of mental and spiritual clarity. It also can be an excellent stone for telepathic communication during the night. It, too, should be dedicated, before sleep, to assist dream recall as well as to gain spiritual understanding through dreams.

PEARLS

Not technically stones, pearls are conducive to dreams.

Pearls are ruled by the moon. They are formed inside oysters, which live in the sea. The moon affects the tides and the creatures of the sea and our dreams as well. The layers of the pearl are deposited in a concentric manner. Their spherical shape, soft luminescent color, and multiple layers are symbolic of the nonlinear nature of dreams. Pearls come from water, but even on land they maintain their connection to the ebbing and flowing and the intuitive nature of the sea.

Pearls from the ocean are more potent for dreams than are freshwater pearls because saltwater is a better conductor of electrical energy. Saltwater pearls are eternally connected with the sea. That alignment allows for a better intuitive connection with your bioelectrical flows. The greater the bioelectrical flow in your body, the more intense and vivid your dreams will be. Having pearls in your dream space will assist you in experiencing intuitive dreams.

CRYSTALS

Crystals have been used since the beginning of mankind as objects of wonder and as a means of understanding and viewing unseen worlds. Their mystique spans time and culture alike.

The scepter of the Scottish Regalia is topped by a crystal globe. Sir Walter Scott said that among the Scottish Highlanders, crystals were called Stones of Power. There are references to the power of crystals in ancient Greek and Roman writings. Egyptians in the eleventh dynasty used crystals for viewing inner dimensions. Shamans in Australia, New

Guinea, Africa, and the Mayan area used these amazing stones. In ancient Japan and China, rock crystals were thought to be the congealed breath of dragons. To the Orientals, the dragon was emblematic of the highest powers of creation. Almost every major culture with an esoteric understanding has used quartz crystals for "seeing."[1]

Native Americans were especially adept in the use of crystals for power dreams. Apache medicine men and medicine women used crystals for inducing visions and finding lost property. Cherokee shamans used crystals for healing, and inner "seeing." Sitting with their crystals, which they regarded as friends, they would burn cedar and offer prayers asking for a dream or vision to guide them.

Many metaphysicians believe that crystals were used for dream work in the lost continent of Atlantis, and that through the use of crystals a person could travel through time and space during his dreams.

Crystals are basically magnifiers and transmitters. They are used in radios. In fact, silicon, which is in the crystal family, is the basis of computer technology. It allows for the processing of enormous amounts of information by transmitting electrical current over its crystalline structure. As there is a bio-electrical current within human beings, we can literally avail ourselves of the power of crystals to "transmit" or enhance dream states by transmitting our intention through its crystalline structure.

USING CRYSTALS TO EXPAND YOUR DREAM STATES

The right crystal. It is preferable to have a crystal that is used just for dreaming and nothing else. A clear quartz crystal that is terminated (comes to a point) on one end is best.

Cleansing. The best way to cleanse a crystal dedicated to dreams is to leave the crystal outdoors on a clear night when

there is a full moon. Place the stone so that the moonlight shines directly on it all night. If this is not possible, try
one of the following:

1. Rub your crystal with eucalyptus oil.
2. Let your crystal soak in water and sea salt.
3. Place your crystal outdoors in sunlight for at least five
   hours.
4. Place your crystal in the ocean or a running clear stream
   for an hour.

Dedicating the crystal. To dedicate your crystal, hold it up
to your third eye and say a dedication, either quietly or aloud.
Program your crystal for only one thing at a time. Some
sample dedications:

> I dedicate you, Dream Crystal, to dreams that will con-
> tribute to my waking life being more joyous.
> I dedicate you, Dream Crystal, to dreams that will
> empower me with a positive vision of myself and a
> strong belief in my own worth.
> I dedicate you, Dream Crystal, to dreams that will enable
> me to develop my unique creative skills.
> I dedicate you, Dream Crystal, to dreams that will allow
> my relationships to heal.
> I dedicate you, Dream Crystal, to dreams that will give me
> powerful insights into my future.
> I dedicate you, Dream Crystal, to dreams that will assist me
> in healing myself and others.
> I dedicate you, Dream Crystal, to dreams that will deepen
> my connection with Spirit.

It is not necessary to dedicate it again. However, if you are
going to change its programming, cleanse and rededicate it.

Dream door. Put your dream crystal in a special place when you are not using it. You can wrap it in black silk to hold the energy, or you can place it in a special spot where you can admire it during the day.

At night, place it near your bed. Just before sleep, hold the crystal to your third eye and imagine that your consciousness is melting into it. Imagine that within it is a mystical door to your dreams. See that door opening. Know that you have opened the mysterious door to your inner realms. Then keep your crystal near you throughout the night.

AMETHYST

The amethyst is in the crystal family. Its rich purple reflects the ability to move easily from one reality to another. The color associated with the third eye is purple, and this magical stone can be used to open the third eye area for spiritual dreams. It is a calming, emotionally balancing stone. As it calms the mind and emotions, our innermost nature can come forth in our dreams.

It is also excellent for people who have recurring nightmares. To use it for this purpose, place your amethyst on your forehead, on the area of your third eye, and program it for deep, calm sleep. It is also an excellent stone to place under your pillow for "sweet dreams."

Dream Pillows

Whether there is some special ingredient in herbs that facilitates dreams or whether it is a behavioral response connecting your dream desire with the aroma remains unknown. The unique scent of the mugwort is thought to open the third eye (the door to dreams). Smelling it while you sleep is not only believed to assist you in remembering your dreams but to reveal dreams of the future. When you sleep with a pillow filled with mugwort, a connection is established between the fragrance of the herbs and your desire for a special dream. What is important is that using a dream pillow really works. Other herbs that can be used in dream pillows are borage, lavender, and yarrow.

The best way to prepare and use a dream pillow is as follows.

- Make sure that the herbs are of the highest quality and, if possible, free of pesticides.
- Use a natural fiber when making the pillowcase. The best fabric is silk, as it is an excellent conductor of bioelectrical energy.

    Wool is also excellent. Many meditators and yogis sit on wool or sheepskin because this helps them align with the bioelectrical energy flows of the planet. Using wool or silk for your dream pillow will help you to experience dreams that are more potent because your bioelectrical energy will be more balanced.

    I suggest using lavender or purple material because these are the colors of the portal to dreams and will contribute to the power of your dream pillow.

- Use your pillow only for dreams so that it is the only thing you associate with dreaming. You might keep it in a special box or covering and take it out only at night, just before bed. The fragrance will then be an intimate reminder of the alignment between you and your dreams.
- Hold the pillow close to your nose as you drift off to sleep. Keep uppermost in your thoughts the desire for a dream. In the morning, deeply inhale the fragrance of your dream pillow. This will usually revive the memory of a dream.

The Chinese Clock

Chinese, Japanese, and Indian cultures have all traditionally thought of time as a nonlinear, circular process (as opposed to the Western concept of linear time). In Chinese medicine, the day is divided into hours assigned to different organs and different aspects of the body.

Gallbladder time is between 11:00 P.M. and 1:00 A.M. It is interesting to note that two of the most potent dream herbs, mugwort and yarrow, are also used to stimulate bile production in the gallbladder. It is not a coincidence that the same herbs used to induce dreams are also gallbladder herbs. Most individuals have their first dream of the night during gallbladder time. In addition to the innate dream-inducing qualities of these herbs, inhaling their aromas or drinking these herbs in a tea stimulates the governing organ (gallbladder) that allows your body to move into alignment with the natural rhythms of the universe. When your body is in alignment with the natural cadence of the universe, you will have more powerful dreams.

If you go to sleep during the gallbladder time, just before going to bed rub your fingers on the temple area above your ears to further stimulate your gallbladder meridian.

Notice what hour you go to sleep, then enhance your dream states by stimulating the corresponding meridian points before sleep.

Fall asleep	**Stimulate**
9–11:00 P.M. Triple Warmer Time (Regulates some of the body's fluids, and is one of the meridians that distributes energy [chi]).	*Rub behind your ears*

11:00 P.M.–1:00 A.M. Gallbladder Time	*Rub above your ears*
1–3:00 A.M. Liver Time	*Rub the area over the liver*
3–5:00 A.M. Lungs Time	*Rub indentions between upper ribs and shoulder*
5–7:00 A.M. Large Intestine Time	*Rub the muscle between forefinger and thumb*
7–9:00 A.M. Stomach Time	*Tap lightly under the eyes*
9–11:00 A.M. Spleen Time	*Circular pressure over spleen, on the left side of the body just below the ribs*
11:00 A.M.–1:00 P.M. Heart Time	*Rub the armpit area of the left arm*
1–3:00 P.M. Small Intestine Time	*Apply deep pressure around the outside base of little fingers*
3–5:00 P.M. Bladder Time	*Rub the area where eyeglasses rest on the nose*
5–7:00 P.M. Kidneys Time	*Rub the center of the sole behind the ball of the big toes*
7–9:00 P.M. Circulation/Sex Time	*Massage middle fingers*

(For more information about how to understand dreams using the Chinese clock method, see chapter 23.)

ANCIENT CHINESE CLOCK

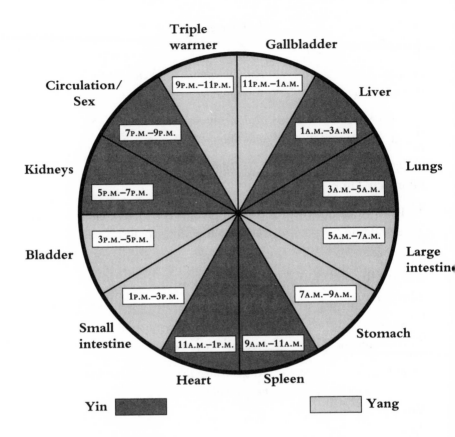

Bodily Alignment

When possible, sleep with your head toward magnetic north. This will better align your bioelectrical energy lines and thus contribute to better dream states.

Food and Drink

Your diet can greatly affect your dream states. If you eat foods that you have trouble digesting, this will contribute to dreams that are "hard to digest." Research has shown that pressure in the digestive system creates restlessness and causes us to wake up with only rambling dream fragments.

If you are properly digesting and assimilating your food, then you will have dreams that you can "assimilate." It is best not to eat immediately before bed.

Melons. These are thought to contribute to vivid dream states. The high water content and round shape of melons suggest an alignment with the moon and the dream realms. Perhaps melons contribute to dreams because they act as diuretics, causing you to sleep lightly and thus allowing you to remember your dreams more easily. Perhaps there is some inherent quality to melons that contributes to dream recall. For whatever reason, they seem to assist some people in recalling dreams. For digestive purposes, eat melons separately from other foods. "Eat them alone or leave them alone" is the current maxim.

Vitamin B6. For some people, taking 50 mg of vitamin B_6 shortly before bed can contribute to dream recall, perhaps because of the diuretic effect of B_6.

Alcohol and other drugs. Alcohol and many drugs repress dreams. The person who regularly goes to bed intoxicated robs himself of restful sleep and dreams. The ancient Greeks, masters of the art of dream interpretation, declared that anyone wanting to enter a dream temple had to abstain from alcohol for three days prior to entering. They felt that clear dreams were difficult to obtain for people who were under the influence of alcohol.

Moon water. Drink water that you have left outside in the moonlight for an hour. Be sure that the moonlight shines directly onto the water, not through the glass. Drink this moon water just before going to bed to contribute to dreaming.

8.

DREAM INCUBATION

*T*he mother crane cautiously peers out through the rushes as the cold Canadian winds whip at the lake, creating strong, uneven waves. Beneath her lie three perfectly formed eggs, warm and snug as their mother protects them from the elements. Sunbeams slant through a dark cloud, a chilling rain falls . . . and the eggs are safe. The evening darkens. The moon's reflection on the water is broken and broken again and still the eggs are safe. Through the long dark night the eggs incubate. The faint light of dawn accents the sounds of water dripping down the marshy reeds. Beneath the mother crane . . . three feeble yet jubilant baby birds.

Just as the crane incubates her eggs to allow them to come to birth, you can incubate your dreams. You can direct your dreams by consciously intending to do so. This idea is not uncommon. We tell someone who is stuck in a problem to "sleep on it." Then, in the morning, as if by miracle, there is the answer that was needed.

Dream incubation is the concept that you can consciously guide the course of your dreams from the wakeful state. For example, a problem presented during waking hours can be resolved during sleep simply by making a conscious choice to do so.

Perhaps you are in a dilemma with one of your children. You might suggest, "Dreams, give me information that will help me resolve the difficulty I'm having with my son"; "Dreams, what would be a valuable career move for me?"; "Why am I having difficulty losing weight, and what can I do to assist myself in this situation?"; "Dreams, I have not been feeling well lately. Is there any specific nutritional guidance that will help me to feel better?" Each of these is an example of dream incubation. You can even ask about previous dreams with regard to specific understanding: "Dreams, why were there kangaroos in my dream last night? What was the meaning of that dream?"

You have heard the expression "sleep on it" in connection with problem solving. Sometimes, putting the problem in the background and getting a good night's sleep will lead to a solution or resolution through a dream. This communication with your dreams can give you answers to many questions in your life.

Almost everyone who studies dreams concurs that they allow us to get in touch with hidden parts of ourselves, tapping wisdom far greater than anything we are consciously aware of. Dream experts differ, however, on the source of the information that comes forth. Some believe it is from a force external to ourselves, such as our guides and/or God. Some are convinced it is our higher self. Other dream experts feel it is simply a segment of our psychological makeup that we are not in touch with during normal consciousness. Nevertheless, through incubating dreams, it has been proven repeatedly that one can receive information that will assist when awake.

It is up to us, the dream makers, to translate these non-physical, nonmaterial expressions into images that make sense in our three-dimensional, linear consciousness. The goal of dream incubation is to create a dream that makes as much sense as possible, that is very clear and understandable.

You can also incubate dreams to test future probabilities. By imagining possible conclusions, you can examine future actions as well as compute the outcomes. This enables you to experience an outcome without actually taking an idea to its completion in your daily life.

When you incubate dreams, it is likely that you will experience profound emotions in the dream state and in waking life. Enjoy your emotions as you would a symphony. Be willing to experience the gamut of your emotions. Allow your feelings to ride the waves of the high and low periods that present themselves to you. Breathe in the excitement when listening to the crescendo and decrescendo of your symphony. Enjoy the anger, caress the sadness, experience the boredom— celebrate each nuance and variation as it occurs. Enjoy all aspects of your dreams; each is an integral thread in the weaving of life.

You can even incubate dreams simply for the enjoyment of it, just as you would enjoy a movie or favorite television show. They need not always be scrutinized for their significant meaning in your life.

If there is an area of your life that you would like to explore, or if you desire a psychic perception about yourself, dream incubation can be valuable. Here are some simple guidelines.

• Choose a time when you are not too tired and have had no drugs or alcohol. Make certain that you will have plenty of time in the morning to process the information given during the night.

• If there is an issue that you want to incubate, first begin to contemplate the specific issue. Consider the solutions already presented and get in touch with your feelings and emotions concerning this issue. Think about what you might need to release if that issue was resolved. Ask yourself, "Am I willing to have this resolved?"; "Am I willing to let go of this difficulty?" Consider how different life would be if that problem was solved. Evaluate the issue from all perspectives.

• Place your dream journal or tape recorder beside your bed. (See chapter 6.) Make sure your spine is straight. As you fall asleep, repeat your request several times, for example: "Help me understand my fear of the dark," etc. Next, imagine that you are releasing all thoughts, attitudes, and feelings regarding that issue. Simply concentrate on your question, repeating it over and over to yourself. If you notice any distracting thoughts, allow them to filter through your awareness, then return to your question. "Dreams, help me understand my fear of flying. Tonight, I release my fear of flying." Hold these thoughts in your mind as you drift off to sleep.

• Incubated dreams usually occur the same night as you request them. Occasionally, however, they will occur the following night. Trust any information that is revealed, even if it appears not to make sense at the time. Write down everything you received immediately upon waking. Be patient in waiting for the understanding. Frequently it is not until the next day or even the next week that you are able to make any association between the dream and the issue from which it was incubated. Nevertheless, within that dream is the answer to your problem or dilemma. Any incubation efforts that you perceived as failures often prove to be quite valuable. Trust that a higher part of yourself has already solved the problem.

Dream incubation is often a valuable tool in releasing relationship difficulties. For example, Alice was given a horse by her father, and that seemed symbolic to her. Consequently, she incubated a dream that would help her to understand what the horse represented. The dream revealed a past lifetime Alice had had with her present-day father. (See chapter 12.) In the past life he had left her, riding away on a horse.

Alice realized that for her, the horse symbolized painful abandonment. As a result of this one dream, she was able to release a great deal of anger at her father. This opened the door for her to create what is now a deep and more loving relationship with her father.

Incubation can be used to receive many types of information. An example of this occurred when I was preparing a new course on manifestation for my seminar curriculum. I had been incredibly busy the week before and had been unable to spend much time preparing to teach the workshop. Early one morning the entire seminar appeared before me in a dream, so I leaped out of bed and wrote down all the details. The information I received was so extensive that I was unable to cover all of it during the day-long seminar.

The idea of dream incubation originated in ancient Greece. Research indicates that there were three hundred to four hundred temples built in honor of the god Asclepius. These temples were in active use for nearly a thousand years, beginning at the end of the sixth century B.C. and culminating at the end of the fifth century A.D.[1] Dreamers would go to a sacred dream temple for the purpose of receiving a useful dream from a god. They believed that by sleeping in holy places and appealing to a god, they could obtain profound answers to their inner questions. To participate in dream incubation now, it is not necessary to sleep in a sacred place or to appeal to a specific god. However, I find that if I honor my place of sleep as an inner temple, and if I appeal to Spirit, both the vivid clarity and the contents of my incubated dreams are enhanced. If possible, locate a beautiful place in nature as was done in ancient times and create a sacred sleep chamber. You might also consider creating a moon ritual. (See chapter 24.) After selecting your form of ritual and purification, call on the Creator or your dream guide to lead you through the night hours, asking for the dream you desire. Ancient Indians,

Chinese, Japanese, Egyptians, Hebrews, and Muslims practiced dream incubation in places of rare beauty found in nature.[2]

When you use dream incubation, anticipate that all your dream expectations will be met. In ancient times the dreamer would participate in purification rites, sacrifices, and other rituals and ceremonies. However, the same effect can be produced if you have a clear intention when you incubate your dream. The manner in which you phrase your dream incubation statement is very important. Instead of, "I hope that tonight I understand why my relationship with my aunt is difficult," say, "Tonight, I understand my relationship with my aunt." Your dreams will respond with clarity proportionate to your intention.

9.
LUCID DREAMING

A narrow pathway, cut like a river gorge,
the path as clear and shining as the river,
winds and turns on its course between the
rocky terrain of waking and the
soft pastures of sleep.
> —M. Anne Sweet

ave you ever been dreaming and then suddenly become conscious that you were dreaming? In lucid dreaming, you are aware that you are dreaming during the dream.

You have probably experienced some degree of lucidity. Perhaps you had a frightening dream, only to find yourself thinking, "Hey, I'm okay, this is only a dream!" When you realize that some segment of your dream is only a dream, it is called "prelucid dreaming." A fully lucid dream is one in which you definitely recognize that you are dreaming. These dreams tend to seem as real and vivid as normal, conscious reality. Also, the senses of sound, sight, taste, and smell seem intensified.

Though lucid dreaming has received much attention from the metaphysical community in recent years, it is not a new idea by any means. Lucid dreaming has always been an element of the spiritual practices of Taoism, Buddhism, and Hinduism.

The Tibetan Buddhists have expanded the practice of lucid dreaming into an art form. They believe that dreaming is a way to connect more deeply with your soul. They feel that each time you dream, you are experiencing the condition of your soul essence, and that if you die while dreaming, the dream will continue. The ancient text *The Tibetan Book of the Dead* gives instructions on how to pass through the different dream dimensions that occur after death. These dimensions are called bardo states. If you are unable to maneuver your way through the bardo states, you are forced to reincarnate into another life. However, if you successfully weave through these dream states, you return to God and total oneness. Obviously, then, lucid dreaming is of the utmost importance to Tibetan Buddhists. They consider it a means to release themselves from what they consider a world of suffering.[1]

The value of lucid dreaming is enormous. When people begin to experience lucid dreaming, the truth of who they really are and their personal reality expand. They begin to feel more expansive—as you do when taking in a deep breath of fresh air—and this feeling begins to affect other aspects of their life. Personal limitations begin to dissolve, and there is a sense of being more in control of personal destiny. Intuition and imagination during waking hours are noticeably increased.

One of the goals of lucid dreaming is to transport your wakeful consciousness into your dreams and your dream consciousness back into your wakeful life without feeling a break. The purpose for this continuity in consciousness is that it allows the dreamer to recognize that the world of the wakeful self is a self-created dream as well. If you are working with lucid dreaming, an excellent affirmation to keep in mind is "All that I see I can dream. All that I dream I can see, and I am aware of all of my dreams."

Lucid dreaming can be regarded as a spiritual evolutionary process, a step toward remembering who you are and what your true destiny is. An Arabic mystic said, "A person must control his thoughts in a dream. The training of this alertness . . . will produce great benefits for the individual. Everyone should apply himself to the attainment of this ability."

Cultivate the skill of lucid dreaming as you would any other skill. Just as the ability to drive, swim, or paint can be developed and fine-tuned with practice, so can the ability to experience lucid dreams. It takes some discipline at first, but it becomes easier, and, in time, effortless.

1. *Lucid dreaming techniques.* As you are going to sleep, say, "Tonight I am aware and conscious that I am dreaming." Use the techniques in chapter 6 to recall your dreams, and as you remember a dream during the night, while you are drifting back to sleep, say, "During my next dream, I remember that I am dreaming." Sometimes repeating the phrase "I am dreaming" several times as you fall asleep will be of help. Having made a conscious choice to experience lucid dreams, be vigilant and consistent. Over a period of weeks, it will begin to happen for you.

2. *Applications.* Once you are adept in this skill, you begin to alter the circumstances of your dreams. Choose some action you can take. Start with something simple. The Mexican mystic Don Juan told Carlos Castaneda to try to look at his hands while he was dreaming. Other simple dream actions could be picking a flower or opening your arms to the heavens in delight or hugging a tree. Give yourself a task to perform in your dreams. You don't need to force your visualization; be in your dream with awareness.

Stanford University psychologist Stephen LaBerge, a proponent of lucid dreaming, has developed sensors that detect the eye movements that accompany vivid dreams. A pulsing red light is then used as a signal to remind the dreamer that he is dreaming and thus help him to have a lucid dream. Though mainstream sleep and dream researchers may be skeptical of this controversial technique, it demonstrates once again the interest being generated for a deeper understanding of our dreaming selves.[2]

10.

DREAM GAZING

I close my eyes and walk down the gentle rolling hill into the valley of my
inner universe, a quiet place for daylight dreaming, a crystal ball through
which I can watch myself move, ask questions, receive answers.

—M. Anne Sweet

*D*ream gazing is similar to daydreaming with an added dimension—it is daydreaming with discipline. It is one way to access the mystical world of dreams through your wakeful consciousness. As you glide deeper into the inner realm, the world of dreams begins to blend subtly with the world of your daily life. Just as it is possible to alter your life through your dreams during the night hours, you can also use daytime dream gazing techniques to alter your life.

In an interview, author Richard Bach revealed the process he used in writing the magical book *Jonathan Livingston Seagull*. Bach described being in a kind of dream state while still awake, wherein he saw a vivid image of a little seagull flying in sunlight. The flash of inspiration gained from this vision grew into the beautiful photos and text of his book. Bach said that he transcribed the images revealed to him while still in the waking-dream state.[1]

Bach was referring to the ability to dream while awake, which I call "awake dreaming" or "dream gazing." To dream gaze, first allow yourself to become very relaxed. Suspend your normal thoughts. Letting them go frees your mind and body to release all tension. Then simply imagine a dream. Create any dream you like, allowing it to be as unpredictable as one that would occur during sleep.

Start with a very simple, one-minute dream. Then, write down exactly what the dream contained. This is especially valuable if you have not been recalling your nightly dreams. You can become familiar with the world of dreams through daytime dreaming.

Another advantage of dream gazing can help you to deal with a difficult scenario in your daily life. You can create or imagine a dream simply by suggesting, "In regard to the situation or difficulty, I am now going to create a dream." Allow your mind to wander freely while you create this dream. Carefully notice the symbols and feelings that begin to well up. This will begin to assist you in resolving your difficult issues. (See chapters 20–29.)

For example, if your elbow is giving you a great deal of pain because of an injury or illness, you, perhaps, might imagine a dream where you are scrambling through a jungle. Suddenly a huge black panther is right behind you in swift pursuit. You leap toward the safety of the dense underbrush, and when you look up, you are looking into the golden eyes of the panther! Without a second's warning, the panther jumps, gripping your elbow in its jagged teeth. You hear the fragile bone snap in two. The pain is excruciating. You are aware of an over-whelming sense of dread and abandonment. You realize you are totally alone. There is no one to help you, no one to whom you can call for help. No one.

To look at this awake dream, write down the details and look at the different aspects of it. First, you are in the jungle. The jungle may represent your primitive nature, your primordial self. The panther is chasing you. Perhaps the panther symbolizes your unconscious, the dark side of yourself, your shadow. You fear encountering your shadow, the primordial reflection of yourself. As the panther rips into your elbow, your elbow seems immobilized. You also sense being unable to move. Perhaps your awake dream represents fear of the primordial part of yourself, which is preventing you from moving forward in life. Perhaps you feel restricted in life because of that fear. As you are nursing your elbow, you are filled with an acute sense of aloneness because no one is coming to your rescue. By beginning to understand the underlying causes of your awake dream, you will likely begin to feel relieved of the problem.

In exploring your awake dream more closely and in understanding its symbolism, perhaps you discover that the fear in the dream represents your fear of moving out into areas that are unknown to you. Then, as you begin to affirm and strengthen your belief in yourself—for example, repeating to yourself something like, "I am able to move into the unknown easily and effortlessly"—you may find that your elbow has greater movement and is no longer in such pain.

For me, dream gazing is a most powerful and useful dream technique. It enables me to move to the very heart of any difficulty and immediately facilitates an expedient resolution.

DREAM WORKERS

Apprentices of subtle craft,
we have gathered much in the following
of this age-worn path:
journeymen to the Loom Masters,
we spin the tapestry,
pictorial odyssey,
crystallized visions,
loving designs of the heart.
                    —M. Anne Sweet

11.

DREAMS FOR "SEEING"

Dream window, throw open the shutters to the sunrise,
a view of the distant road to be traveled, an event
far, far away; but something tells me I must
start closer to home, the garden waits to be tended.
                                        —M. Anne Sweet

*J*raced down the beach, sharp stones cutting my feet, tears stinging my face as the wind whipped at my clothes. A thunderstorm marked the sky with jagged scars across dark clouds. Finally, I fell to the ground, sobs of anguish and anger wrenching my entire being. I clutched at a cold, sharp rock, and squeezed it until its edges cut my hand. With every heaving breath, I wanted to die. I had been betrayed.

I cried until there were no more tears within me. Empty, vacant, I got up and walked home. As I lay in bed, a dense fog of loneliness suffocated me. I had never felt so alone. Gradually the gripping tension lessened, and I drifted off into a restless sleep.

Hazy, dark shadows slipped in and out of my dreams . . .
homeless specters aimlessly wandering . . . forever in the chasm

99

of the night. In the distance, I could see a brilliant light. As I was drawn to its soothing glow, shrouded, formless beings tugged at my arms. Wrenching away from their bony grasp, I glided gently to the light, its beacon a welcome relief to my hollow heart. Face and form elude memory, but my awareness still retains a feeling . . . and a voice. "You are to weep no more. You have passed the second barrier and you will never need to return this way again. I am with you . . . I am with you . . . I am with you." The sound of the voice echoed within me, resounding with strength and power as it gathered energy much like that of an approaching storm.

Slowly the image faded, and I fell into a deep, sweet sleep. I awakened feeling so refreshed. The night's storm had cleared the sky and sunlight filtered softly through my bedroom window. I stretched and reached to touch the light, caressing its liquid warmth on my fingers. I felt so new. Something had lifted during the night. My fear had melted and there was an awareness of the beginning of a new day. Something mystical had occurred during the night hours. Someone had come and soothed my aching soul. At this crossroads in my life, many years ago, a visitor, vaguely familiar to me, pointed the way . . . and it made all the difference.

Most people can recount at least one dream that provided them with a new understanding of life or that helped them during a crucial period. These dreams appear to reach beyond the ordinary boundaries set by most dream analysts. They are monoliths speaking of an ancient wisdom and a deeper magic. These were the prophetic or visionary dreams of old. They originate from the wellspring deep within us, where God resides. These dreams are not necessarily ordered or commanded but reach out to us in times of need. They lend assurance and guidance through the "dark night of the soul." The prerequisites to tracing the thread that leads to vision and prophecy are an open heart and the willingness to ask . . . and to listen.

Visionary dreams are different in character from precognitive dreams. A precognitive dream allows you to glimpse the future. Dream researchers state that these dreams are fairly common. Even Freud reported cases of precognitive dreams. One thoroughly documented case is the story of Clinton H. Elliott.

Back in the mid-1950s, Elliott dreamed that his sister would die in a matter of six weeks, which, in fact, she did. What was most amazing about this was that it added credence to his claim that he had dreamed he too would die soon. When he received this message, he informed his family and friends and began to put his affairs in order. He calmly made plans for his family's future. He even told his wife the kind of funeral he desired. At age sixty-six, death was easily a possibility, except that he was remarkably healthy. He spoke of his coming death to his friends and co-workers. He was employed in the construction of a tunnel being built under Boston Harbor. Although his belief in his impending death might have contributed to a slow, dwindling death, this was not the case. Elliott died by accident—a very strange accident. He was at his worksite, discussing his future death with the other construction workers, who, needless to say, were a bit skeptical. As Elliott finished his shift, an enormous crane, which had been checked thoroughly by the safety inspectors less than an hour before, suddenly collapsed, killing Elliott immediately. It was a totally unpredictable accident to everyone except Elliott. He had dream-predicted his death.[1]

Almost all death dreams indicate psychological release or death of old beliefs rather than actual physical death, but in this case Elliott *was* able to see the future through his dreams. Dreams with prophetic import have often led to historical consequences. The Duke of Wellington was inspired to restore the Alhambra in Spain as a result of a dream in which he saw this beautiful Moorish palace disintegrating. President

Roosevelt declared that Washington, D.C., needed a new airport, because he had had a disturbing dream that foretold an accident due to the disrepair of the existing airport. Cornelia, the wife of Caesar, had a prophetic dream of her husband's death and tried to forestall his attending the fatal meeting of the Roman Senate.

Often, our personal guides give us information in our dreams. However, there are also disseminating guides, who, rather than work with only one individual, serve a purpose similar to broadcasting. When an idea whose time has come emerges, these guides begin broadcasting that information. People who have their psychic antennae tuned to that "station" will receive the information. This is exactly why inventions or discoveries occur at the same time in several parts of the world, often within days of one another. When people are sleeping, they are less mentally defensive, so they are more receptive to the information being broadcast from the psychic realms. Hence, many discoveries have their origins in dreams.

Often, dreams are a means for those who have died to communicate with us. It seems easier for us to hear them through our dreams. It is usually more for our sake than for theirs. Usually there is something that we have not completed in regard to this individual, perhaps something that we didn't communicate, that has become a stumbling block for us. The visitation will often clear up those blockages. There are occasions, however, when there is some message or warning that these departed ones feel that we need to hear. Keep in mind, however, that just because someone has died, it does not necessarily mean that he or she has grown in wisdom. If someone is lacking in wisdom when he is alive, he possibly will continue this way when dead. So, remember to weigh the advice that is given against your own good judgment.

If you need to resolve an issue with someone who has died, or you feel a need for his comfort or solace, "call" him just before drifting off to sleep. The way to do this is to feel that you are touching this person's essence. Allow yourself to experience the connection you had with him while he was alive. As you are going to bed, hold his essence close and ask him to come to you during the night. Doing this can help to ease your loneliness when someone has gone.

Some individuals have remarkable alien encounters during their sleep and the number of this type of dream is increasing. Even now, many best-selling books and top-grossing movies concern aliens. Either we have become more receptive to their tentative venturing, or they are becoming far more persistent. For whichever reason, the UFO phenomenon is here to stay and will become increasingly prevalent in our lives and play a more significant role in our dreams. For the most part the alien beings that appear in dreams offer valuable advice and guidance. However, remember that though they might come with lovely, lofty messages, first and foremost you should follow your own inner guidance.

There are very specific methods to increase your ability to have psychic or "seeing" dreams. The first step is to incubate for your dreams. (See chapter 8.) You can incubate for visionary dreams, precognitive dreams, past life exploration, astral travel, or to enter the realm of fairies and angels.

Whether these "seeing" dreams are "real" or the figments of a collective consciousness is irrelevant. The value comes from the experiences you have during the night. Ask yourself:

Are the messages gained from these dreams valuable?
Do they contribute to my waking life?
Do they expand my inner horizons?

Any dream that allows you to look into the future, view the past, communicate with loved ones who have passed on, gain a vision, or even enter into other dimensions is a "seeing" dream. These special kinds of dreams expand your horizons into the realms beyond ordinary perception of reality. They allow you to reach below the surface of the human mind, to the place where the world is not made of separate parts but it is seamlessly joined in a rich tapestry of interrelatedness. In the deepest sense your "seeing" dreams allow you to step beyond the confines of your life experiences into a much more profound arena. These kinds of dreams are like holograms where an entire object can be reproduced from a small part of the hologram. A "seeing" dream may contain the innate structure for a larger segment of life. They are special dreams that allow us to expand our sense of self from the restriction of a limited point in time and space into a much more vast universe of awareness.

I'm often asked how can you tell if a dream is a precognitive one or just a psychological balancing of inner concerns. The following criteria have assisted me greatly in making this distinction.

How to tell if a dream is precognitive:

1. The dream is in color or the colors are unusually vivid. A precognitive dream isn't always in color, but it can be one of several determining factors.
2. You will get the message in three different ways during the dream. The message may appear in three separate but distinct forms within one dream.
3. There will usually be a round or circular object within the dream. This can be a ball, a round plate, a circular mirror, and so on.

If a dream that seems precognitive fits all three criteria, there is a very good chance that it is a foretelling dream. Sometimes you will get a precognitive dream with all the criteria and yet interpret it incorrectly. The following letter is an example of this process.

Dear Denise,

The following is what I believe was a prophetic dream. I used your method of dream interpretation to decipher this dream and it met all three requirements of a prophetic dream: 1. There were three parts. 2. It was in extremely vivid color. 3. It contained a significant object that was round.

I had been interviewed for a different job within my company a few weeks before this dream and I was awaiting further developments. This is the dream; it was in three parts:

> *First, I dreamed that I received some news about a job. I was quite excited about it. Then there was a sudden change. In the second part of the dream I was in an office. A couple of men, who were my new bosses, were talking. I looked down and noticed I was wearing a hideous pair of trousers. They were bell-bottoms with green, black, and white striped designs. I was extremely embarrassed and tried to make myself inconspicuous. I wanted to change into another pair of trousers without the men seeing me. In the third part of the dream I was in a big gymnasium. There was a huge piece of paper covering the entire floor. It was my new job to fold and unfold the paper into different configurations, like origami, the art of Japanese paper folding. My co-workers and I created various shapes by folding them. One of them was a huge round hoop or a ring shape.*

I was awakened by the telephone ringing. It was my mother informing me that the office wanted me to come in for a second interview. She had been calling repeatedly but I had not heard the phone.

As I drove to the interview, I was thinking this was going to be a piece of cake. I was sure I had the job because I so clearly had had a prophetic dream in which I got a new job. The interview was difficult. The guy asked technical questions that I was unable to answer, and he cut me off every time I tried to tell him about myself. I remembered feeling embarrassed by the entire situation.

A week later I found that I hadn't gotten the job. When I heard that news, I thought maybe it wasn't a real prophetic dream after all, but later I realized that I just hadn't interpreted it correctly. In the first part of the dream I received news about a job. That happened. I was called in for the second interview. In the second part of the dream I was feeling inadequate and self-conscious, which is exactly the way I felt in the interview because I could not answer the technical questions the interviewer asked me. The paper-folding part was a little more obscure but that part was also prophetic. My search for another job is a large, convoluted task. I keep turning opportunities over in my mind, pulling them apart and putting them together in various ways, symbolized by my folding and unfolding the paper.

I learned from this dream that the obvious interpretation might not always be correct, especially when I am too attached to the interpretation. I was so excited about the interview that I jumped to conclusions and did not take time to listen to my feelings or really study the dream. I thought you'd be interested in hearing this dream.

Shine on Brightly,

Karl

The way that Karl learned from his dream, including the realization that he was trying to fit his dream to his expectations, was a valuable lesson. Dreams for "seeing" will allow you to expand your inner horizons, and as you do so, your outer boundaries will also expand.

12.

DREAMS FOR PAST LIFE RECALL

As I travel through this lifetime
swimming down the stream,
I pick up many baubles,
people, places, things.

The one thing I'll take with me
when it's time to leave the stream,
isn't any bauble, it's
my pocketful of dreams.

—Karl Bettinger

*T*he gondola gracefully swayed through the soothing waters just off the coast of Venice. The oars-
man bellowed off-key arias as we gently glided past
one island after another. One particular island seemed to
glisten more brightly than the others in the distant haze. As I
pointed the island out to my singing host, he gently headed
the gondola toward it. This beguiling gem in the sea seemed
to beckon mysteriously to me.

As I stepped onto the dock, a slightly balding, round Franciscan monk rushed to greet us. He spoke some English and
offered to give me a tour of the entire island, which consisted

of the Franciscan monastery and its grounds. As I followed his jolly form, I was swept away by an overwhelming feeling of déjà vu. I was so comfortable on the island. I felt as if I knew exactly what was around each corner, even before we reached it. Images and forgotten memories flooded my consciousness. How could I know my way so clearly? I had never even heard of this island. Suddenly, as we rounded another corner, I viewed a scene far different from the one I was "remembering." Unable to help myself, I blurted, "Oh, this is new!" With an astonished, look the monk replied, "It is new to the original structure . . . but it is more than six hundred years old." To my amazement, I had unearthed memories of being a monk on this lovely island over six hundred years before. Thus, my journey into past life exploration began.

Have you ever had the experience of being in a foreign place and sensing a familiarity too uncanny to describe? Have you ever listened to a particular piece of music and instantly found yourself transported to another time and place? Perhaps you have met a stranger and experienced an instant rapport that you didn't understand, or you've met someone new and taken an immediate dislike to him or her. Have you had a dream in which you found yourself in a foreign place, or in foreign clothes, and yet experienced a tremendous sense of familiarity? It could be that you were being reminded of someone or someplace from your childhood long forgotten, or it could be that you have lived there before. Perhaps you were in that foreign town in a different body, in a different time. Could it be that you knew that stranger in another existence—in another incarnation? Could dreams be a key to past lives?

The concept of reincarnation was known long before recorded history. In fact, over half of the people in today's world believe in reincarnation. It is the idea that the soul is eternal and, as such, returns to the earth plane again and again, through rebirth in various bodies, in order to grow and learn.

Each lifetime provides experiences that allow one, as spirit, to become stronger, more balanced, more loving, and, eventually, to unite with God.

In one life, you may live in poverty to learn humility and resourcefulness. In another lifetime, you may be extremely wealthy to learn to deal with money fairly and in a positive manner. In one life, you may be blind in order to learn inner sight, and in another one be athletic, enabling you to experience and fully understand physical strength. You may be a woman in one life and a man in another, or be Caucasian in one and Asian in another. Past lives are not so much building blocks as they are a jigsaw puzzle, with each life contributing to our evolution in becoming whole, complete, and balanced.

"As ye sow, so shall ye reap." This is the law of karma. Karma is the fate we create for ourselves as a result of our actions in this lifetime as well as in previous ones. The idea of karma gives us a clearer understanding of why one individual may experience adversity throughout his or her entire life while another has an easy path.

Reincarnation and karma provide us with a clearer picture of our purpose and mission in the present, through our understanding of previous lifetimes. They also give us a better understanding of our destiny in the universe. Life is not a onetime affair, nor is it a series of meaningless experiences strung together haphazardly. Rather, it is a mystical ongoing journey that allows you to emerge as a conscious, loving being. The search for your soul may be the most important work you have ever undertaken.

Throughout history, celebrated philosophers have pondered the vast mysteries of life, death, and rebirth. The first record concerning reincarnation was discovered in ancient Egypt. Those ancients believed the soul was immortal; when the body perished, the soul entered another human body.

The ancient as well as the present-day Hindus believe that the soul is immortal and inhabits one body after another in search of its true divine nature. In the centuries preceding Christ, Buddha shared wisdom regarding the cycle of reincarnation, the great wheel of life and death. Buddhists, similar to the Hindus, strive to be released from the death/rebirth cycle by attaining nirvana, or oneness with God. The Essenes, an early Jewish sect, are also said to have believed in reincarnation.

In 500 B.C., the Greek philosopher Pythagoras wrote of reincarnation and gave descriptions of his personal recollections of his various incarnations. Plato also believed in reincarnation and the continued evolution of the soul. Napoleon Bonaparte once admitted to having been Charlemagne in a past life. Voltaire, the French philosopher, observed, "It is not more surprising to be born twice than once." And the Spanish painter Salvador Dali confessed that he was the great Spanish mystic St. John of the Cross. Even such diverse New World personalities as Benjamin Franklin, Ralph Waldo Emerson, Henry Ford, Walt Whitman, Henry Longfellow, Henry David Thoreau, Thomas Edison, and General George Patton ascribed to the teachings of reincarnation.[1]

Benjamin Franklin, in one reference to past lives, wrote his own epitaph, which has since been titled "the most famous of American epitaphs." It reads as follows:

The body of B. Franklin, Printer,
like the cover of an old book,
its contents torn out and
stripped of its lettering and
gilding,
lies here, food for worms, but
the work shall not be lost.
For it will appear once more
in a new and elegant edition,
revised and corrected by the
Author

There are many excellent books on the subject for those who are interested in seeking proof of reincarnation. My purpose here, however, is not to refute any doubts regarding past lives, although I firmly believe in them. Rather, I intend to illustrate that your dreams can serve as a doorway to your past. By stepping through that door, you may expand the quality of life beyond your expectations.

The value of discovering your past lives is immeasurable. Spiritually exploring past lives and other dimensions is a way to tune in to inner guidance and leads to personal integration. You find yourself more often in the right place at the right time. Some develop a strong relationship with their guides, while others experience spontaneous spiritual awakenings.

To release psychological problems without exploring the source beneath the symptoms is like attempting to kill weeds with a lawn mower. The problems will come up again and again until one dissolves the roots that created the difficulty. Someone who eats compulsively may discover that in another life he or she starved to death and that fear has now resurfaced as an insatiable desire for food. By experiencing a past life either in your wakeful or dream state, you can begin to release the decisions made in past lives that are affecting you today.

Children are especially adept at recalling their past lives in the dream state. When my daughter was eight years old, she shared with me a remarkable dream in which she was a black man during the time of slavery. She described in detail how her trousers were ragged at the edges and how she tilled the soil with a dilapidated hoe. She confided that some of her present-day friends were also black slaves in that lifetime. Perhaps one of the most curious factors regarding this experience was that one of her friends, whom she had seen in this dream, had had a similar dream in which she was also a black slave in the South.

In order to connect with your past lives during sleep, it is important to utilize the variety of techniques described in chapters 6–10. Each evening repeat to yourself before retiring, "Tonight, I dream of a past life." Continue to repeat this phrase as you drift off to sleep. When you first begin, you may find that you receive only a wisp of a memory that could be from the past. To receive more clarity, during your waking hours use your imagination to expand what you have received, regardless of how insignificant it may seem. For example, let's say you saw an ornate helmet in one of your dreams. When you wake, imagine the kind of person who might have used that helmet. Imagine where he might have worn it as well as the circumstances of his life. Imagination is an invaluable resource in discovering your past.

Imagine a past life associated with your dream images, and more often than not you will begin to see who you once were. Often, individuals who have obtained vivid past-life dreams have actually traveled to one or more of the places they experienced in their dreams and have discovered that their dream perceptions were accurate. Past-life recall can be fun in the dream state and enormously rewarding in your daily life.

13.

DREAMS FOR ASTRAL TRAVEL

Body abruptly whipped away, leaving my spirit
to be caught and drawn up by a current of thought;
heart and spirit soar on the wings of an eagle,
plunging dives, circle then uplift again on warm winds.
— M. Anne Sweet

I soar, frolic, and gallop with ecstasy to the lofty ceiling of my bedroom, and then dive for the comfort of my soft teddy bear. With a burst of glee, tumbling and twirling, I soar to the ceiling once again with reckless abandon, taking a moment to hover over my rag doll's cradle. My mother opens the bedroom door. "What are you doing, Denise?" she asks. Innocently I respond, "Oh, nothing, Mommy." "That's nice," she murmurs and closes the door. Only momentarily disturbed, once again I am jumping off the bed, arms outstretched, my body careening wildly through the air.

When I was a child I was always leaping off the end of my bed, tumbling and flying through midair. I really believed that I could fly. I didn't know that I was experiencing astral travel. As I got older, I forgot the ability to fly consciously. In my

113

dreams, however, there were relics of this memory. Occasionally I would discover myself in a dream soaring over the rooftops and racing to the stars. In my twenties, I enrolled in a week-long course on astral travel. There, I reclaimed a degree of the skill that had given me such joy as a child.

Astral travel is one category of dream experience not included in the definitions of dreaming or lucid dreaming. It is commonly referred to as an out-of-body experience. This is when your spirit is literally separated from your physical body, and it usually occurs during sleep. Numerous esoteric religions and philosophies are based on this experience. In addition to a sense of separation from the physical body, there is a self-awareness that is extremely vivid that accompanies astral travel. This is quite different from a dream, though it is not uncommon. In fact, during sleep, the sensation of a quick jerk may be indicative of a difficult astral reentry into your body. We often have out-of-body experiences, yet fail to recall them.

Dreams of flying or of being in an airplane frequently accompany out-of-body experiences. Also, people who actually fly, such as pilots, in their waking life are often inclined toward out-of-body experiences. Research indicates that people who as children believed they could fly, or liked to jump off trees or roofs, also have a tendency toward out-of-body experiences.

There are records of such experiences occurring throughout history. Descriptions of these experiences are similar whether they took place in India, Egypt, South America, or even in the midwestern United States. Vivid out-of-body experiences are frequently triggered by an accident or a near-death experience.

In rare instances, they are generated by a deliberate, conscious attempt to leave the body. Most people find that these experiences dramatically alter their beliefs concerning the nature of personal reality. They also tend to be extremely joyous experiences. The authenticity of these experiences can be verified. Specific studies reflect that at least twenty-five percent of adults recall having had at least one out-of-body experience in their lifetime. Many did not realize that they were having out-of-body experiences until the phenomenon was defined for them.

There appears to be no research indicating that damage results from consciously leaving your body. In truth, it is a very natural occurrence. It is interesting to note that when you are having an out-of-body experience, you do not experience time or space as you generally do. Another interesting phenomenon is that you may notice, when you first leave your body, that you seem to remain very much in your present physical form. However, the longer you are separated from your physical body, the weaker that sensation becomes, and your "being" appears to transcend into a cloudlike vapor or some other amorphous substance.

There are certain variables that seem to influence the out-of-body experience. Alcohol appears to be a definite deterrent to experiencing this phenomenon. One thing that seems to slightly increase your ability to leave your body is the way you position it, particularly if you lie in the north–south direction with your head to the north. The north–south alignment is also valuable in regard to deep sleep. If you desire a very restful night's sleep, placing your head toward the magnetic north is ideal. However, if you want to feel energized, placing your head toward the south works best. For astral travel, your head should be toward the north.

In a book by Carlos Castaneda, Don Juan, Castaneda's mystical teacher, instructed him in the arts of lucid dreaming and astral travel. Don Juan maintained that when one had mastered the techniques of dreaming, there was no longer any difference between the things one did while asleep and while awake.[1]

Oliver Fox astral traveled extensively and wrote about his astral experiences. He said that the scenes he encountered were more beautiful, glamorous, and mystical than anything he had ever seen while awake. He described his sensations as exquisitely enjoyable and said that his mental state was one of extraordinary clarity, power, and freedom.[2]

When I began astral travel, I remained close to my home. I observed myself wandering through the rooms in our house. Curiously, my traveling would often be in a different time frame—it would be daytime instead of night. The astral dimension is an arena that is outside the space-time continuum. As I gained more confidence in this area, I began to experience floating and, eventually, flying. At the start, I would venture only a few feet above the ground because I still feared that my physical body would fall. As I grew in confidence, I felt the ecstasy of flight.

My first adult recollection of astral travel was a frightening one. It was a very humid night in Hawaii. Early that evening, I spent time with a good friend, casually discussing the art of astral travel. Neither of us had experienced it. We jokingly agreed to meet each other at 3:00 A.M. and selected a location. Before I retired, I said to myself, "Tonight, I will meet Susan at 3:00 A.M. by the waterfall in the upper Manoa Valley."

At about 3:00 A.M. I awoke, aware of a very strange sensation. Although the room was dark, I felt a kind of rocking, floating sensation, as if I were drifting on a rubber raft in a swimming pool. I was startled. The ceiling, which was normally six to seven feet above my bed, was now only inches from my body. I was weightless . . . without substance. What was this? What was happening? I couldn't understand why I was hovering so near the ceiling. Was it a dream? I was fully conscious, and it seemed so very real. I was so light, so free. Then, almost as an afterthought, I rolled over gently and noticed that my bed was below—with me in it! The terror of seeing my body was so great that I immediately zoomed back into it with a harsh jolt. The shock was so profound that it was a long time before I ventured out again.

It was as if I had split into two different people. The part of me that I identify as "who I am" was free, light, and floating. The other part, which I associate with my physical body, was somehow me but not me, lying on the bed, a mere physical shell. This was the first of my many explorations into the nature of astral travel and out-of-body adventures.

History has given us many examples of astral travel. In the first century A.D., the writer Plutarch told of a soldier in Asia who, while unconscious, roamed for three days in another dimension. Native tribes have always taken out-of-body experiences for granted. American Indian shamans and African witch doctors have practiced rituals enabling them to escape their physical bodies. The Australian Aborigines would go into a trance and venture out on an astral journey whenever their tribes needed guidance. This was shown in the movie *The Right Stuff*, when the Aborigines were assisting the astronaut as he was maneuvering his space capsule. Legends from prehistoric days share the secrets of those who left their bodies and communicated with the gods.[3]

Even churches, throughout time, have recorded out-of-body experiences. Saints such as Anthony of Padua and Alphonsius Liguori were seen elsewhere while their physical bodies remained in a church or monastery. The scientific mystic Emanuel Swedenborg visited many dimensions, scripting detailed accounts of what he had seen. Thomas De Quincey reportedly left his body while smoking opium.[4]

It is said that Napoleon, shortly before his death, traveled astrally from St. Helena to Rome to inform his mother that he was dying.[5]

The British Society for Psychical Research, formed in 1882, studied astral travel and other psychic phenomena. Richard Hodgson, William James, Sir Oliver Lodge, and others from the society investigated many of these cases. A number of universities throughout the world are now involved in research in this field. Out-of-body experiments have been designed in which the sleeper astrally projects to another building and then describes what he sees during his visit.[6]

Many out-of-body experiences are described by soldiers during war when they have literally leaped out of their bodies to escape the horrors of gunfire or other explosives. Occasionally, people leave their bodies simply to visit a friend or a family member. A mother will travel to see her daughter; a father, his son. St. Augustine related the story of a man lying in bed who suddenly looked up to see a philosopher friend standing in his room. They began to discuss Plato. When the two men met the following day the man inquired about the experience. The philosopher responded simply, "I did not do it, but I dreamed that I did."[7]

In *On the Delay of Divine Justice*, Plutarch tells about Aridaeus of Asia being knocked unconscious and immediately taken from his body. While out of his body, he saw his uncle who had died years earlier. His uncle greeted him, assuring Aridaeus that he was not dead and that his soul was in fact firmly attached to his body. "The rest of his soul," explained the dead uncle, "was a cord connecting it to the body. So long as the cord still remained attached to his physical body, Aridaeus would still be alive." Aridaeus also saw a marked difference between his double, or his astral body, and the astral body of his dead uncle. His body had a faint shadowy outline, while his uncle's was transparent. While observing this phenomenon, Aridaeus suddenly became aware of being "sucked through a tube by a violent inbreath," and he awoke once again to find himself back in his physical body.[8]

This tube is similar to the tunnel that many astral travelers experience when they are leaving and returning to their physical bodies. The astral body has different names in different cultures. The Hebrews call it *ruach*. In Egypt, it is known as *ka*. The Greeks knew it as *eidolon*. The Romans called it *larva*. In Tibet, it is still referred to as the *bardo body*.

In Germany, it is *Jüdel* or *Doppelgänger* or *fylgja*. Ancient Britons gave it various terms: *fetch*; *waft*; *tisk*; *fye*. In China it was *thankhi*. The *thankhi* left the body during sleep, and their records indicate that the astral body could be seen by others. Ancient Chinese meditated to achieve astral travel. They believed the second body was formed in the area of the solar plexus by the action of spirit, and that it then left through the head. Many of these ancient Chinese teachings were discovered on seventeenth-century wooden tablets describing the phenomenon of out-of-body experiences. The ancient Hindus called this second body, the astral body, *pranamayakosha*. Buddhists referred to it as the *rupa*.[9]

Anthropologists studying various native tribes have found that astral travel is a very common event. The cultural beliefs of the astral traveler determine the pattern of his or her experience. In eastern Peru, the shaman imagines he is leaving his body in the form of a bird. Asian tribesmen view the silver cord, spoken of by modern metaphysicians, as a ribbon, thread, or rainbow. Africans perceive it as a rope; the natives of Borneo, as a ladder. Regardless of how the phenomenon is defined, it appears common among astral travelers that a type of silver cord remains as a connection between the astral and physical bodies.

The scientific view of these dreams is that they are ancestral memories from the days when, according to Darwin's theory, our predecessors were aquatic and airborne creatures. Psychologists refer to astral dreams as a type of depersonalization, or a means of avoiding being grounded in normal reality.

Conditions of Travel

In order to experience astral travel, there are two very important prerequisites. The first is that you believe and appreciate the reality of an astral body. The second is that you believe that you can do it and specifically focus your desire on leaving your physical body. If it were an easy thing to accomplish consciously, astral travel would be an everyday occurrence. However, I believe that anyone can experience the existence of an astral body if his or her intent is great enough. In any case, most of us do experience astral travel. We simply don't remember it. If we strongly identify with our physical rather than our astral bodies, it can be a frightening experience. The greatest barrier we encounter is fear itself.

FEAR

Even the most fearless of us will discover, upon deeper examination, that at some time we have come face to face with the wall of fear. First and foremost is the fear of death—the fear that if we are separated from our physical body, perhaps we will die. Our automatic reaction may be to get back within the physical body quickly, because this is where our life is, in the physical. We tend to have this reaction in spite of our emotional attitudes and our intellectual thought processes. Only after repeating the experience many times can we hope to release the fear of death. It is much like beginning to swim and eventually realizing that your body will float, that you will not drown.

Another common fear is "Will I be able to get back into my body?" I can say with absolute certainty that you will do so. There is abundant evidence that those who experience astral travel are always able to return safely. Fear of the unknown is also faced by many astral travelers. There is no guidebook. The healthiest way I know is to work through your fear simply by allowing it to exist while still being willing to explore the unknown.

Astral Aids

Following are some guidelines to assist you in your astral journeys. The first thing to do is relax. You might take some stress-reduction courses or read about creative visualizations to help you to relax completely. You might also try self-hypnosis or posthypnotic suggestions. A visit to a hypnotherapist may assist you in this. Meditation may also help you move into a very deep state of relaxation. Placing your head toward the north and straightening your spine will also make a difference.

The next step is to move into the space between wakeful and sleep consciousness. This is a very delicate balance. It is where you are not yet asleep but are no longer awake. You might focus on an image or symbol that is special to you. As you move more and more into a deep state of relaxation, begin to observe the kind of mind pictures or any light patterns that appear randomly. Frequently these are referred to as neural discharges. Do not encourage or deny them, simply allow them to move through, acknowledging an even deeper state of relaxation while maintaining conscious awareness. Perhaps you will recognize that you are deepening your consciousness because your body will begin to feel either extremely heavy or light. Your senses of touch, smell, and taste will begin to fade. Occasionally, your hearing will also begin to fade.

As you are in this very calm, relaxed place, with your eyes closed, focus your awareness outside your body. Begin to imagine that you are now at some point outside your body. If it is in another corner of the room, imagine that you are touching the wall. Be aware of the floor and all objects near you. Imagine that you are in this place. Often, as you begin to leave your body, you will experience a tingling sensation or hear a vibration. At this point, it is crucial simply to allow the vibrations to increase in frequency. This will occur until the frequency is so high that you will be almost unable to perceive it. Your body may feel slightly warmer.

The last step is to imagine that you are moving your hand. Imagine yourself reaching out for and touching any object that is near, while remembering that this is not your physical body but your astral body.

Another way to enhance what you are doing is to imagine gently pushing against the wall. Then begin to increase the pressure. At this point, it will appear as if your hand or arm is actually going through the wall. Then carefully withdraw your hand.

The ancient Etruscans took part in a rolling technique where they would enter into a very deep state of relaxation. They would imagine rolling out of their bodies as a means to leave the body for astral travel. Some travelers prefer a lift-out method, where they imagine floating up out of the body.

The important thing is that you experiment, discovering which method works best for you. Be gentle with yourself. Sometimes after long periods of practice without attaining any results, in that moment when you least expect it, you will experience your first out-of-body journey.

Returning to Your Body

Once you have learned to leave your body, you are free to explore and examine anything and any place you desire. When you wish to return to your body, simply imagine moving either your fingers or your toes in your physical body. This will bring your spirit back into your body immediately. You can also swallow or move your jaw to bring yourself back. A simple guideline is to activate any one of your five senses, and this will return you to your body.

14.

DREAMS FOR HEALING

My thin cotton summer dress rippled in the warm wind as I stood high above the vast blue sea. I felt exhilarated as I stretched my arms toward the sky. I turned from my vantage on the chalk-colored cliffs that overstretched the sea and barefooted my way through the golden grasses. A lone seagull circled overhead. His slow-cycling shadow whispered over the undulating grasses that moved in response to the ocean breeze. In the distance was a black cottage. There were no windows or doors. It was completely black. Like heat radiating off a hot road, its image seemed to waver like a mirage in the distance. As I approached the black cottage, I was aware that there was someone inside. Sue. It was Sue inside! "Sue, come out! It's so beautiful out here!" Inside I heard the timid feeble response, "I can't come out."

"Please, Sue," I urged. "It's so dark in there. You must come out into the light." There was no response, only the distant sound of waves greeting well-worn rocks below chalk-colored cliffs.

I awoke from my dream. It seemed so real. I felt exhausted. That was the tenth time I had had that dream in as many days.

Sue, a vivacious woman in her early thirties, was dying of

cancer. Initially, when I was called in to contribute to Sue's healing, I was astonished to see this once-hearty woman reduced to a mere ninety-eight pounds. She was as frail as a skeleton, with stretched-taut skin over her bones and deeply sunken eyes and cheeks. Every day I went to Sue's bedside to assist in her healing process, and every night I met Sue in my dreams. I assumed that my purpose in these nightly healing sessions was to encourage Sue to step into her own healing. On the eleventh night I dreamed:

> *I'm standing outside the black cottage. As usual, the radiant rays of the sun bathe the summer grasses with fluid golden light. I place my hands on the peeling black paint of the cottage. "Sue. Please, Sue, come out." A solemn, hollow voice from within replies, "I can't come out. My husband is here."*

I assumed that she was attempting to tell me, through this dream, that she had a suppressed emotion concerning her husband that was preventing her from healing. Thinking that I might have discovered the source of the cancer, I began to work with Sue on undelivered communications concerning her husband. I thought this must be the path to her healing. We worked in depth on all difficulties regarding her husband that she felt were unresolved.

Sue continued to get weaker. This was hard for me to accept, because everyone with whom I had ever worked had improved and regained their health. I often contributed to the healing of those whom the medical profession felt were incurable, frequently with miraculous results. What was I doing wrong?

> *I stood on the chalk-colored cliffs inhaling the essence of the slumbering sea below. As I walked through golden grass, I could feel the warmth of the earth radiate up through the soles of my bare feet. The black cottage seemed to shimmer in the sunlight like a mirage of a desert oasis. I once again urged Sue to venture*

out into the light. Sue responded, "I'm not quite ready. My husband is keeping me here."

Sue's husband was constantly at her side. He seemed never to leave her, even for a moment. Sue began counting the days until Christmas. She had two beautiful children in their early teens and she desperately wanted to celebrate Christmas with them. She had to live until Christmas. The day after Christmas, the nurse asked Sue's husband if he would leave the room so that she could change the bedding.

In that moment, when he left the room, Sue's spirit soared . . . and her body died. That night, again, I dreamed.

I stood barefoot, on towering, majestic white cliffs. The ocean had never seemed more radiant . . . more magical. It seemed to hold the very essence of life, the womb of all beingness. Shimmering diamonds of light danced on the ocean's surface. The air was heavy with the fragrance of sea and foam. I became aware of a serene presence standing beside me. Turning, I was greeted by a softly swirling goddess of light. "Sue?" I looked in the direction of the black cottage. There was only the vast horizon. I had seen Sue only when she was ill and emaciated. The woman beside me was completely whole and radiated an exquisite beauty. This lovely woman said, "They think I am dead. I am so alive. If only they knew. You see, Denise, death can be a healing as well. I am healed and I am well."

In that moment, I realized that it can be as healing to assist someone in dying as it is to assist someone in living. In my nightly urging for Sue to step into the light, I was making it easier for her to release her physical form. She had completed her incarnation and was ready to move on. Her husband's attachment to her had been holding her back. In the moment that he left the room, she went for the light, leaving her body behind.

Sue allowed me to see a deeper aspect of dream healing—an aspect that contributed to my daytime healing practice as well. Many people practice dream healing every night. Most are unaware of doing so. Often, those who have incarnated to participate in dream healing will reincarnate around battlefields or other areas where there is a great need for healing. These beings help the dying to make the transition from living to spirit. In war-torn areas of Europe during World War I and World War II, there were a large number of dream workers who were assisting the wounded and the dying to step into the light. They helped make that transition easier.

Dream healing can contribute not only to the dying but to the living. Frequently, knowledge of our cure lies deep within our psyche, too deep to access during the daylight hours. A dream healer can contribute to another's healing simply by touching deep within the psyche in sleep. The rules for daylight healing apply to night healing as well. Gaining an understanding of these tenets of healing will contribute to your intention to join the ranks of the healers of the night.

Asclepius, called the Father of Medicine, was believed to work his cures during sleep. He would appear in his patients' dreams, mix potions, apply bandages, and, at times, summon snakes to come and lick their wounds or infected areas. The very symbol of modern medicine, Hermes's staff, is a configuration of two intertwined snakes. Dream healing is a very powerful way to heal yourself and those you love. However, before learning dream healing techniques, remember these very important tenets in regard to healing.

WE ARE ALL HEALERS

Within each of us resides the ability to heal. When we remove the considerations and the doubts, each of us can tap in to that gift. A common concern among those who are first entering the field of healing and dream healing is whether they know enough or have enough experience to heal anyone. My old Chinese teacher used to say that a person will draw to himself those who want what he has to offer. So, whatever your level of ability, whoever comes to you knows, within his higher self, what you have to offer. And what you have to offer is what that person needs at that time. Do not doubt this. You have within you right now all that you need to heal. You already know enough.

WE ARE NOT OUR BODIES

While this appears obvious to many, there are those who do not realize that it is upon this premise that great healing occurs. The body is an illusion. Remember that you are not just working on the body or even on the astral plane or the emotions. Rather, become aware of the spiritual essence of another.

While it is possible to heal another person by deciding what is wrong with him or her and "fixing" it, a more powerful way is to realize we are not bodies; we are infinite, immortal, eternal, universal beings. Find that place that is universal within the person with whom you are working. Go beyond the idea of separation and find that place of oneness and connect to it. Remember who both of you truly are in that moment. There will be healing. The essence of true healing is oneness.

BELIEF SYSTEMS AFFECT HEALING

It is not necessarily the method or technique in itself that heals. Most techniques can work. Rather, it can be your belief or your faith in the technique that will heal. For instance, it is common in Western cultures to "believe in" the practice of medicine by the medical profession. Many people put their faith in their doctors and in this way have found the place where they can best heal themselves. However, in cultures where native healers are prevalent, often a traditional healer can gain better results than a western-style doctor because of the prevailing belief system.

THERE ARE TWO KINDS OF HEALING—
CAUSAL AND SYMPTOMATIC

In symptomatic healing, the healer can assist in elevating or focusing on the symptoms. However, unless the true cause is addressed, the person with whom you are working can find the problems recurring or may develop other difficulties.

For example, if a young man has arthritis in his right hand, perhaps the underlying cause can be traced to earlier experiences with his father. If, when the boy was young, his father smacked the backs of his hands when he was misbehaving, consider the range of emotions in play. While feeling enraged, the boy also loved his father, yet feared him. Perhaps the child began to deny those feelings and just felt overwhelmed and powerless. He might have felt that he couldn't get a handle on what was happening to him. Now, as a grown man, when he finds himself in a situation where he feels helpless or powerless, where he can't get a handle on things, his hands are affected.

A symptomatic healer, using the dream state and various dream techniques, can help the man gain freedom of movement and relief from the pain in his hand. However, unless the young man can release the underlying feelings of powerlessness, the arthritis can return, or some other difficulty will manifest iself in another area of the body.

In other words, it is important not to think there is something "wrong" with someone and attempt to fix it. A more powerful way to heal is to see the divinity in that person and know that he or she has the capacity to heal from within. The healer who sees the individual as he truly is can work with the cause of the difficulty and can help facilitate healing.

THE BODY REFLECTS CONSCIOUSNESS

Every emotion or thought that a person has ever had remains stored in the body, as do all the emotions that were denied or suppressed, and these influence the health and well-being of the body.

Normally, as a person goes through life, situations arise that can cause him or her to feel angry, sad, joyous, and so on. When that person decides that it is inappropriate to have the emotional response that he is beginning to experience, he can "go numb" or deny what is happening to his body. He can find some way *not to feel* whatever is going on with him. Each of these unexperienced emotions can create physical difficulties. These are the body's way of putting attention on what needs to be cleared.

When there is a health problem, the emotions and situations that caused the difficulty are usually not those that have been experienced or felt. Rather, the problem arises from situations that have *not* been experienced: those situations where a person went numb, or didn't allow himself to feel the pain, or grief, or anger. Individuals then tend to create similar circumstances again and again, even lifetime after lifetime, until finally they fully experience what has been avoided.

ALL HEALING IS SELF-HEALING

The body always wants to heal itself. No technique or method in and of itself ever healed anyone. It is the body's response to that method that heals. Two people with the same difficulty can be given identical procedures and one will be healed and the other will not. This happens because all healing is basically self-healing. The person with whom you are working heals himself. You are the facilitator.

THE ONLY PERSON YOU EVER HEAL IS YOURSELF

The true essence of healing is oneness, and the greatest healers know that when they are healing others they are also healing themselves. Each person with whom you work is a part of you. It is "you" in a different body. This is a universal law. Know that each person you have drawn to yourself for healing is a different aspect of your own being, for we are not separate from each other.

For example, if someone in your life has cancer, one way to start the healing process is to look first within yourself and ask, "Is there anything 'eating away' at me?" As you begin to heal the emotions that are eating away at you, the healing process may begin within the person you want to heal.

My kahuna teacher said that it was a sacred thing and a great honor to be allowed to contribute to the healing of someone else. If you want to contribute to someone's healing, and that person is having difficulty receiving, then look within yourself. First, allow yourself to know that *you* deserve love. Open yourself up to the deepening of this awareness. As you create that context for another's healing, you heal yourself.

As a healer, and particularly as a dream healer, you must not feel that you are sacrificing yourself. You must know that you are not better than the people whom you are healing. You are healed through helping them to heal.

In any kind of healing, it is important to go beyond the feeling of separation. Reach that exquisite level of oneness. Remove any walls that you sense between yourself and another, so that you feel the unity that is between the two of you.

DISEASE AND/OR PHYSICAL DIFFICULTIES CAN BE A GIFT
Physical difficulties can be a way of learning. If the healer prematurely removes blockages before the higher self of the ailing person has learned whatever he needed to learn from the imbalance, it will be re-created. It is important to provide a safe space for the person to choose his or her path. It is not for you, the healer, to arbitrarily make that decision. Ulti-

mately, you do not know what is best for another. It is not appropriate for you to decide what is wrong with someone and then "fix it." This response is associated with belief in the illusion that a person is just his body. We are not our ailments.

LOVE IS THE ULTIMATE HEALER
One aspect of the definition of love is unconditional acceptance of another's reality. This acceptance is at a deeper level than personality or persona. When you move into absolute acceptance of another's very essence, then there is nothing more you need to do to bring about true healing. Your presence is enough.

HEALTH IS A FUNCTION OF SERVICE
Service is *not* seeing that someone else is in bad shape and deciding to help him. This idea of "fixing" him comes from forgetting that he is divine and in the process of choosing his reality. It also sets you up as seeing yourself as better than he is. It implies that you will help someone up but not quite "up" as far as you are. Allow people to go beyond you, and you will grow. This is true service.

My Chinese teacher used to say, "It is a poor student who doesn't surpass his teacher." Hanuman, the monkey god of India, said, "When I don't know who I am, I serve you. When I know who I am, I am you."

Do what you can to contribute to the world so that it will be a better place—not for the world's sake, as the world may be perfect just the way it is, but for your own sake. In the same way, do what you can for another, for your own sake, remembering that the essence of the person is perfect as he or she is. Don't sacrifice—ever. True service is not sacrifice.

A HEALER IS COMPASSIONATE
As a healer, you must maintain a balance by having one foot in the reality of the physical world and the other in the realm of spirit. In the spirit realm, you know that the world is

perfect. In this realm you know that there are no accidents and that each person has generated his or her own illness and is responsible for his life. However, by remaining in intense spiritual focus, you may become cool and lack compassion for the suffering of others. In contrast, by focusing intensely only on the physical world, you become a player in a large drama. In this reality most people get caught up in the misery of the world and begin to feel sorry for others. We forget that others are not their bodies or their problems. It is easy to get into this frame of mind and fail to see beyond the suffering. But if we do this, we have forgotten who we really are.

It is important to be compassionate and to sympathize with another's pain, yet to remember his or her true essence. The person is not ill; it's the body that is ill. Find this balance and you will be an excellent healer.

INTENTION

Once you understand these tenets of healing, you can begin to enter the realm of dream healers. The most important aspect of night healing is your intention. As you prepare for sleep, be relaxed and comfortable. Use the dream guide technique or the dream shield technique (see chapters 17 and 18). Let your full intention be to contribute to the healing of the person you have in mind. To do this, first imagine him or her very clearly. If you are not visual, get a sense of him. (Each person has a unique feeling or aura.) Get in touch with the person's feeling. Hold his essence. Say his name within yourself. You might even visualize him as very happy. See him running, jumping, feeling exhilarated. Then go to sleep. Where intention goes, energy flows. You may not remember what good you contributed during the night; nevertheless you will have begun to move into the realm of night healers.

Often, my clients tell me that they have been aware of my working with them in their dreams, and on waking have discovered that their symptoms are relieved. Occasionally, I will have no recall of having visited them in the night, or I will have only a faint glimmer of a memory. I have even told individuals I would work with them in the night and then have forgotten to program myself before bed, only to hear the next day how effective the night healing was. So, don't be discouraged. It might be that you have been a night healer all along.

If you want to contribute to your own healing, as you go to sleep say, "Tonight I am healed. Tonight I am healed." Your body can heal itself through your dreams. Your soul may be trying to communicate a very important message through your illness or disease. Use your dream state as a workshop to receive these communications, and thus help you to heal.

15.

DREAMS FOR LOVE
AND SEX

He moves with confident grace as he saunters down the beach. His back muscles ripple with feline certainty as he takes long, languid strides. He hesitates . . . and turns to face me. We are no longer two strangers who happen to be walking in the same direction on a lonely beach. We have entered into a conspiracy of attraction. The look is brief. It is only the suggestion of a glance. Still, in that silent moment, a tangible current fills me with his soul. I walk on . . . and smile.

I woke up from this dream feeling a mysterious inner glow. My encounter with my dream lover had been so brief and yet so fulfilling. I sang through the entire day.

Dreams can be a pathway to ecstasy. They can be a way to expand love of others and of self and can be used to work out sexual difficulties within daily life. They can even be a wonderful form of evening entertainment.

Sexuality appears regularly in the dream state. Men have erections frequently during the REM states, and women's vaginas moisten during these times. It is a normal, natural part of the dream state. In ancient cultures, there was an understanding of this natural occurrence. In fact, the under-

134

standing of sexuality and sensuality was considered basic to
the expression of all life. In the East, it was a means of
expressing unity with Spirit. Sexuality was viewed as a path
to mystical experience. An ancient Indian text states,
"Sexual union is an auspicious Yoga which involves enjoyment of all the sensual pleasures and gives release. It is a Path
to Liberation."

In the Orient, it was thought that the underlying reality to
all of life consisted of two dynamic energies, called yin and
yang. Yin was the receptive, feminine principle and yang was
the masculine, outgoing energy. Each was considered necessary for harmonization of life. Yin was embodied in the
receptive energy of the moon. Yang was embodied in
the projecting energy of the sun. Everything was considered
either yin or yang, and all life was an interplay between the
two forces.

Human beings were considered the highest expression of
these two powerful dual energies. A healthy sexual union
was considered a way to break through the illusion of
duality—a way to attain liberation and to enhance health
and well-being. Sexual union was a way to become closer to
God, and dreams were considered a powerful arena in which
to experience and express one's sexuality. Dream sex can
provide you with spiritual experiences, deep insights, and
light-hearted fun, but first you may need to overcome guilt
about your sexual dreams.

Guilt

When you have dream sex, it is common to feel guilty about
it. Thus, it is important to know that there is no cause for
guilt in any dream relationship. In all ancient cultures that had
a metaphysical basis, sex was not considered in conflict with
spirituality or religion. Sex was both an art form and a normal

part of each person's education. It was important that sexuality was not shrouded in guilt.

In dreams, there is no such thing as incest or promiscuity. Your dream lovers are simply different aspects of yourself appearing in erotic form. In addition to letting go of guilt over dream sex, it is important that you work on releasing any guilt carried from past sexual activities. This guilt can be subconsciously activated every time you have sex. To experience full sexual union in the present, it is essential to forgive yourself for your past. When you believe that you are guilty and your source of guilt lies in the past, you are not looking inward. To look inward is to know that everything that you have ever experienced was necessary for your growth and understanding. It was necessary for you to be who you are today. Even the thoughts and actions you may be ashamed of contributed to your being who you are. As uncomfortable as those memories are, it is important to observe and release them. Work on forgiving yourself and others, and make amends if needed. Any guilt that you cling to can create barriers for you. It is often processed and released in your dreams.

Whenever you feel the pain of guilt, remember this: If you yield to it instead of forgiving yourself, you are deciding against inner peace. Therefore, say to yourself gently but with conviction, "I accept who I am and what I have done as well as what others have done to me. I accept and forgive myself." This may not be enough, as some guilt is deeply rooted, but it is a good beginning.

One valuable technique is to write down all feelings of sexual guilt, then burn the pages, saying, "I release now and forever my attachments to this guilt. So be it." Your dreams can reinforce the releases that occur in your daily life as a result of this process.

Opening the Dream Sex Channel

Another important aspect of sexuality is the understanding of
how energy flows through the body. Within the body are
energy centers called chakras. In order to maintain a healthy
view of yourself, it is imperative to have a harmonious circulation of your life force energies through the chakras. When
these energies become blocked, self-esteem is lowered, disease
occurs, and vitality diminishes. Basic to this energy flow is
your sexual energy, which can be likened to your creative
energy. Often, people involved in a spiritual movement deny
or block this vital energy, and they become so "heavenly"
that they become ineffective in their earthly pursuits.

We need to maintain a balance within all our chakras in
order to be empowered in day-to-day life. The first chakra,
the sexual center, is important to the maintenance of all the
others. It is our connection to the earth. It is the home of
the kundalini, that mysterious force dwelling at the base of the
spine that yogis strive to awaken. It is what is referred to in
the Orient as the "fighting spirit." This doesn't imply that you
should pick a fight. It simply refers to zest and vitality for life.
As this area opens, women discover that their menstrual flows
become easier, hormones are vitalized, skin becomes softer
and clearer, and they are rejuvenated. You have probably seen
a woman who seems illuminated by her own glow. This is
usually a woman whose first chakra is open and clear. When a
man's first chakra opens, he will feel more empowered in his
life and will operate from a perspective of greater clarity and
certainty. You do not need to have sex to have your sexual
energy open.

Each of our chakras represents a different facet of ourselves,
and each deserves to be developed and opened. However, the
first chakra is one easily ignored by those on a spiritual path,
because of guilt or denial. Your sexual energy is part of your

God-given heritage. Use it. Allow it to open, and your sensuality and your zest for life will increase.

One method to prepare for dream sex is to channel the
sexual energy upward through the chakras to the top of the
head, which in India is known as the aperture of Brahma.
This can be done with the use of breath. Eastern mystical
teachings stress the importance of breath as a way to align and
channel creative sexual energy. Your breath should be slow
and deep, extending your lower abdomen when you inhale
and contracting it when you exhale. This is the most natural
way to breathe. It is the way we breathe when we are asleep.
However, most people breathe just the opposite, with the
chest expanding on the inhalation. Once you've mastered this
type of deep breathing, imagine a brilliant surge of energy
entering at your feet, moving up through your entire body,
and exiting at the top of your head. This exercise will begin to
open your chakras, which often leads to enlightening, transformational experiences during sleep. Sexual dreams sometimes indicate the rising of the kundalini, and many major
enlightenments occur as a result.

Once you experience this energy moving through your
entire being, you might want to do the dream lover meditation on page 168. You might also fall asleep repeating expressions such as, "This night, show me the highest potential of
sexuality. Tonight, let me dream of divine intimacy."

Dream Sex and Creativity

An active sex life in dreams not only contributes to a sensuous
waking life but indicates self-actualization and confidence.
Abraham Maslow, the noted American humanistic psychologist who presented the idea of self-actualization, said that
people with potent sexual dream lives are usually self-assured,
independent, composed, and competent. The dreams of a less
self-assured person are more likely to be symbolic rather than

the openly sexual dreams experienced by the person with high self-esteem.[1]

One researcher discovered a strong correlation between sexual dreams and creativity. In a creative writing class, the instructor divided students into groups of the most creative and the least creative, based on writing assignments. Then data was collected from both study groups. The noncreative students had sexually passive or nonsexual dreams. The more creative students had a higher proportion of overtly sexual dreams. The researchers concluded that freedom of sexual activity in dreams is related to freedom of creative thinking in all areas.[2]

Interpretation of Dream Sex

Occasionally, women dream of having a penis. Freudian analysts call this "penis envy" and believe that these dreams imply a secret desire on the part of the woman to have a penis. However, these dreams can represent the woman's desire for achievement of traditional male characteristics that they may see symbolized by the penis.

However, certain dreams of sex are wish-fulfillment dreams, especially those portraying extremely satisfying sexual encounters when the dreamer has gone a long time without sex. Occasionally, these dreams can literally revolutionize a person's sex life. In some dreams, one may experience making love with an individual of the same sex (or the opposite sex in the case of a homosexual). This isn't necessarily latent homosexuality or latent heterosexuality. Rather, it is most likely a desire to attain those qualities represented by the lover. For example, if a woman dreams of making love with another woman who is very strong, it may reflect her desire to incorporate qualities of strength into her own character.

In analyzing your dream, notice where your sexual encounter takes place. For example, a sex dream that occurs in a Victorian house may symbolize Victorian attitudes. If you are having sex in the basement, perhaps you are experiencing submerged or subconscious feelings concerning sex, or maybe your dream is indicating some area of sexuality that you consider crude or base. If your dream encounter is in the middle of a raging hurricane, this generally indicates that you are experiencing powerful emotions with regard to your sexuality.

Dream Sharing

One special aspect of dream sex is dream sharing. You can literally share a dream with a loved one. This exercise is enhanced when you sleep together, because your auras are so intermingled. It is then easier to step into each other's dreams. Dream sharing can also be done from a distance. If you are separated from your loved one, it can be a way to continue your intimacy. To experience the most effective dream sharing, it is valuable to discuss it beforehand. Mutually agree to enter each other's dreams. As you go to sleep, affirm, with intention, that you and your partner will be together in your dreams. Often, dream sharing occurs without preprogramming. Perhaps you have shared a dream with your lover. The following morning, you discover that you both experienced the same or a similar dream. Dream sharing can be an excellent way to increase intimacy and to develop greater understanding in relationships.

Before beginning your dream sharing, it is valuable to do a simple meditation. The following one is based on a Tantric Buddhist technique.

First, sit in a comfortable position directly facing your partner. Make sure your spine is straight. This is extremely important for this meditation. Now, begin the natural deep breathing described on page 138. Remember, as you inhale,

your abdomen expands, and as you exhale, it contracts.
If you sense your chest expanding and contracting instead
of your abdomen, simply imagine the presence of a balloon
in the center of your abdomen. The balloon expands and
contracts with each breath. It may take a short time to
become accustomed to this type of breathing; however, the
results will be well worth it. It is a very natural way of
breathing; this is the way you breathe when you are asleep.
Allow yourself to feel very relaxed. Then, imagine a current
of energy originating in the center of the earth, moving up
through your spine, all the way up through your entire
being. This is your grounding cord. Imagine this energy
moving out of the top of your head like a geyser, then
cascading around you like a fountain. Look into the left eye
of your partner and imagine a beam of energy flowing from
your heart chakra (the energy center in the middle of the
chest) into the heart chakra of your partner. Then imagine
this same energy moving down his or her spine and
penetrating the sexual chakra. This extremely potent energy
then travels from your partner's first chakra area into your
own and moves back to your heart chakra once again. This is
called the "circle of gold technique." You may also reverse
the flow of the energy. As you are doing this, allow yourself
to experience the very deep and profound connection with
your partner. Once you have completed this exercise,
maintain silence and go to sleep immediately, programming
yourself for an even deeper connection during the night.

16.

DREAMS FOR CHILDREN

Children, still close to the knowledge of their souls,
play hopscotch in the schoolyard, leaping over
dragons and dungeons, one foot, two feet grounded,
finishing every battle victorious, unscathed.
                              —M. Anne Sweet

golden pool of melted butter floats in my morning oatmeal. My finger, finding a chip in the earthen bowl, idly plays with its rough edges. My ten-year-old daughter is in the middle of an engaging conversation concerning her exploits of the night before. I am enjoying our family's breakfast dream sharing. When Meadow shares her dreams, a hazy look crosses her face as she vividly remembers the intimate details. Her dreams are usually long-winded sagas full of intricate details. They sometimes appear to span generations. She also pays close attention to details in her daily life. David's dreams are usually succinct and to the point—much like his personality. My dreams are usually active and whimsical.

When we take time to share our dreams and assist one another in understanding their secret messages, the quality of the day is more balanced. For each of us, our dream sharing is extremely significant for the consolidation of our family energy. It provides Meadow with a sense of acceptance and a deeper understanding of herself. Meadow claims she is more apt to recall her dreams and use their messages when we take this time to share our dreams over breakfast.

It is not uncommon that when a child relates a dream, an adult will nonverbally communicate that dreams are not to be taken seriously. When a child has had a nightmare, we rush to reassure him, saying, "Oh, it's just a dream. It doesn't mean anything."

Listening to your child's dreams, even in the middle of the night when you are longing to crawl back into bed, can have an inspiring and transforming effect on your child's life.

Dream Importance

It is important to communicate to your children the significance and value of their dreams. You want to encourage your child's interest in dreams. Never, ever, correct or criticize the child's behavior in the dream or belittle any of his or her feelings concerning the dream. Let your children know you enjoy hearing about their dreams exactly as they occurred. Many children need to be encouraged to confront the beasts or other scary things in their dreams. Teach your child that it is all right to call on his dream guide or guardian angel to help him out of a threatening situation.

Savanna, one of my daughter's friends, told me that she was afraid to go to sleep at night because she thought scary monsters would come in the dark. I gave her a pointed quartz crystal I had programmed for use as a dream crystal. I told her that as she went to bed, she should hold the crystal in her hand and say out loud, "I command that all dream monsters leave now!" Savanna later informed me that since using the dream crystal, she has not experienced any nightmares and sleeps peacefully through the night.

It is valuable for a child to feel empowerment through dreams. Let your child know he can have control over his dreams. If your children have difficulty feeling powerful in dreams, and they have already attempted to change their dreams, without success, it is important to continue encouraging them. Your children may feel worse about themselves because they have been unable to change a dream. If this occurs, have them either act out or draw the dream with a more powerful ending. Your emphasis should be on the flexibility and changeability of dreams. Listen carefully and attune to what your child needs in the moment.

Also, let your children know that they can use dreams to develop a talent or ability that can then be incorporated into their daily lives. They can say to themselves before sleep, "I'd like to become a better swimmer, skater, or artist. Give me the dream that will help me accomplish this goal."

Dream Books

To help your child with his or her dreams, obtain a "dream book" in which your child can record dreams. It can be a notebook, scrapbook, diary, or even a few blank pages stapled together. Allow your child to select the book that most appeals to him or her. Explain that this is a special book to be used only for dreams. Children can write the dreams themselves, or, if they are too young, you can write the dreams for them. Then, have your child create a drawing of the dream alongside the story. Your child may want to make a picture of how he was feeling or how he wished the dream had ended.

The dream book can also be utilized when children think of additional stories regarding their dreams. If they had a disturbing dream, they can go back into the dream and rewrite it, making themselves the hero or heroine. Help them understand that it is all right to go back into the dream and have it end exactly the way they wished it had. Let them know that even scary things in the dream can be changed.

Dream Interpretation

It is crucial for parents to give their children enough time and space to interpret their dreams. It may be difficult at first for children to figure out what their dreams mean. Simply by allowing them to share their dreams, you will empower them in their daily lives. As you talk about the interpretation of your dreams, your child will feel safer in talking about his ideas of what his dreams mean. Dream guidance should be very gentle, and children should never feel that they are being pushed.

Nightmares

If your child has recurring nightmares, you can help by giving him crayons and paper and encouraging him to draw the object that scares him. When a child draws the monster or scary creature, he can put it in jail, make it look silly, or even draw a dream guide that is bigger and more powerful. With this simple exercise, the nightmares often cease.

Dream Champions

If your child is having difficulty in either scaring off the monsters or believing that he or she can change any part of a dream, you may wish to become a "dream champion" for your child. By becoming a dream champion, you actually begin to fight the battle for your child in an improvised drama until he either feels safe or feels empowered enough to take over the battle for himself. For example, you can hold an imaginary sword in your hand and say out loud, "Now I have the sword in my hand; the hairy monster is backing up. Look how afraid he is of this bright sword! I am so powerful that the monster is starting to run away, but I won't let him just run because the magic silver in the sword is going to destroy him so that he never comes back to scare you again!" If at any point in the drama you can give the imaginary sword to your child, do so. I find that once the child feels safe and has some sense of control, he will often want the sword and will "finish" the job himself.

Dream Sharing

One delightful way to introduce children to learning about their dreams is for them to have a "dream visitation" night. Recently, my daughter invited her friends Savanna and Roslyn to spend the night. These eight-year-olds had never done any dream work previously. Just before they went to bed, I said, "Tonight, why don't you all share your dreams. Tonight, why don't you enter one another's dreams." Following is what occurred as told in their own words.

ROSLYN'S DREAM

Savanna and Meadow and I were walking to a rock shop. Savanna had brought her best crystal. I had brought an orange crystal I found on the way. Meadow had brought a crystal she had found near her home. When we got to the rock workshop, everyone was cutting crystals into quarters. We sat down and started to cut ours into quarters. Savanna was very mad because she had brought her best crystal, but she did it anyway. We cut them and then we had to glue them back together. Little chips were falling out. We were to glue those back in, too. When we got done, we took our crystals and wrapped them up in paper and took them home. Savanna still had her best crystal, but it wasn't like it used to be. It still had little chips out of it that she had forgotten to glue back.

SAVANNA'S DREAM

Meadow and I were sisters. There was a man who had kidnapped a girl. I told Meadow about it. Meadow got so mad she threw him in the swimming pool. Roslyn was watching. Meadow was mad because she liked this man and he had been pretending to be nice to her.

MEADOW'S DREAM

[A condensed version—Meadow's dreams are epic novels.]

A few days ago, two of my friends were spending the night and my mom said, "All of you girls are to share a dream." It didn't seem like we all shared the same dream, but we all dreamed about each other and I am going to tell you one of the dreams I had that night:

I was with my friend, Savanna, eating at her school cafeteria, and she started punching into the principal's computer. I found myself and her, in the principal's office, punching all these things into his big computer. Savanna remembered that the principal had all these rules like, "You'll have to die if you mess with the principal's computer." Then she remembered that we had to stick our hands in a window thing. We stuck our hand in this window, but when Savanna tried to pull her hand out, something grabbed her hand with all these bones on it and pulled her in. I grabbed her foot and pulled her out. The principal began chasing us. We ran through all these things through the whole school. We had to do all these things or die. We finally got out.

Roslyn was there and all three of us ran to the town square. I asked them, "Do either of you have a quarter?" They said, "No." Savanna said, "A quarter is a lot of money!" I ran up the hill to town and called her mother, Sandra, to see if she could come and get us. And for some reason, I was becoming quarterless during all this. Finally, my mom came and I told her the story about the principal, how he was chasing us. She started videotaping him and becoming friends with him. She was kind of the hero of my dreams because she made the principal all happy and then he forgot about chasing us. And then my mom picked me up and asked me how my day was and I said, "Oh, nothing exciting." And then Savanna and Roslyn were picked up by Sandra. Everyone was safe and happy at the end of my dream.

[Meadow's note: "I think the meaning of this dream is to go ahead and take chances and it will have a good ending. Take chances in life."]

It was interesting to note that not only did the girls recall their dreams, but each dream had all three girls in it. Without going into any in-depth interpretation, it is fascinating to note that two of the dreams (Roslyn's and Meadow's) had the idea of quarters in them, and two of the dreams had the idea of a male protagonist who was eventually overcome.

Meadow asked if she could relate a dream that she felt was very significant to her. I have included it because it demonstrates a method of dealing positively with a child's nightmares.

MEADOW'S NIGHTMARE
A month or two ago, I had a dream about robbers and this man, who used to be my mom's friend, was one of the robbers. I was so

horribly terrified. That is my biggest fear—robbers, coming in and taking things and being there. It was probably the most scary dream I ever had and I was really frightened.

And then, after talking to my mom about that dream I got really scared just talking about it. So, she put out a pillow and she said to pretend that that was the robber, so I began chopping him and hitting him with my hands and beating him. Then, the next night, I had another dream about robbers in the house. But this time I had a plan. If we heard the robbers knock on the door, at the count of three, we would open both doors—the back and the front doors. We had it all figured out. I woke up and I was a little scared, and then I thought about killing the robbers, so I wasn't scared. I think that was a really good improvement, don't you?

Then right after that, I had a dream that me and my mom were where this man lives who had been the robber in my first dream, and we saw this beautiful house. And, that is where he lived. And my mom said, "Oh, it's so nice to be back again." And, I wasn't mad at this person anymore and he wasn't a poo-poo head anymore. So, I think I've really changed through my dreams.

By showing Meadow that she could be in control of her dream states (i.e., by hitting the "robber" pillow), she was able to feel more powerful than her dream enemy, and this feeling carried over into her daily life. Meadow is no longer afraid of robbers.

> The man in the moon looked out of the moon
> Looked out of the moon and said,
> 'Tis time for all children on the earth,
> To think about getting to bed.
> —Mother Goose

DREAM MEDITATIONS

*To become Loom Master is to weave
with the threads of the universe,
the thread of a thought,
of a breath on the wind,
drawn from the earth
from the moon and the stars,
a textile so fine, it is the
gossamer clothing of our souls.*
                —M. Anne Sweet

17.

DREAM GUIDE

*T*he three meditations contained in this section are inward journeys that you can either read to a loved one or tape record and play back to yourself before sleep. The first meditation will allow you access to the assistance of a dream guide. Dream guides usher people through their dreams, assisting them in transporting gifts of wisdom back from the "other side." A dream guide is an entity who can guide you safely through the night and help you to glean greater understanding of yourself and the inner dimensions. Your guide may be someone you knew in a past life or one whom you were with in your present life who has passed on. Your guide might even be an angel or divine being providing guidance during the night.

DREAM GUIDE MEDITATION
You are about to embark on an exciting journey to that place within yourself. Once you have tapped in to this inner place, you will have access to an inner source of great strength, power, and peace. You are starting a journey where you will encounter your dream guide.

To set out on this journey, lie or sit in a comfortable position. Uncross your arms and legs, get as comfortable as possible.

Do this now. Good.

As soon as you are completely comfortable, allow your eyes to close softly. Now inhale. Completely fill your lungs with air . . . hold for three seconds . . . and as you exhale, feel yourself relaxing.

Take another breath . . . even deeper than before . . . hold . . . exhale completely . . . and experience your entire body relaxing. Now, one final deep breath. Hold for three seconds and relax.

Good. Now focus your attention on your left foot. Feel your left foot relaxing. It is now completely relaxed. Focus your attention on your right foot. Feel your right foot relaxing. Your right foot is now completely relaxed. With each breath you take, feel yourself deliciously, pleasantly relaxing.

Now focus your awareness on your left leg and feel your left leg relaxing. Feel it completely relax. Allow yourself to be aware of your right leg and feel it relaxing. Be aware as your right leg totally relaxes. Now imagine a warm wave of relaxation rolling up from your feet, extending up through your legs, your abdomen, your chest, up to your shoulders, down your arms, and all the way out through the tips of your fingers. Imagine one warm wave after another. Good.

Imagine your abdomen is a balloon. As you inhale, the balloon inflates. As you exhale, imagine you are letting the air out of the balloon. As the balloon slowly, slowly deflates, you become even more relaxed. You may do this now. Good. Your entire body from the neck down is now relaxed, warm, and comfortable. Now focus your awareness on your neck muscles, allowing your neck to relax. Feel your jaw and face relax . . . completely relax.

Now, imagine yourself in a beautiful, natural environment

on a star-shimmering night. It may be by the ocean or among the silent spaces of trees in a lush green forest, or at the peak of a lofty mountain with the moon glistening off the snow or an enchanted meadow filled with fawns, fairies, and unicorns. It may be a place you have been before or a place that exists only in your imagination. It is whatever is beautiful to you . . . whatever makes you happy and comfortable in being there. Do this now.

Imagine this moonlit, starry place as thoroughly as possible. Spend some time seeing yourself and experiencing this environment, using all your senses. Listen to the still sounds of the night. Imagine yourself walking, running, dancing, and exploring in every way this special environment. Make it as real as possible by using all your senses; create it so you can feel it. Use your senses of touch, smell, and sight. Good.

Now, somewhere in this natural environment, imagine a still pool—still . . . deep . . . serene . . . clear. This is a quiet pond with moonlight secrets hidden in its depths . . . a spring-fed pool where you can see your reflection, but altered as if in a dream. Its surface is satin, glass-clear water . . . still water. This water is dedicated to your intuition, your clarity, and your dreams. Take just a short while to really visualize the water. Then, as you are observing this still pool, begin to notice a mist that is forming over its surface. The mist grows, beginning to swirl and dance as if it has a life of its own. Whirling, twirling, and dancing, the mist reaches out until the entire environment is wrapped in this mystical fog. You feel totally comfortable, safe, and serene.

As you stand bathed in the moonlit comfort of this mist, your intuition gently informs you that someone is approaching in the distance. As you sense the presence coming closer and closer, you are aware of great strength, power, and radiance. A calm serenity radiates from this being as he or she comes closer . . . and still closer. You await this arrival with anticipation. You experience a connection with this being as your guide continues to make his or her way into your presence. Through the mist, you can feel in every cell of your being the pervading love and absolute, unconditional acceptance that is given to you by your guide.

Your guide is coming forth to provide you with insight, to give you assistance through the night, to allow you to access your power and perfection in the waking hours. And now your guide is coming closer to you, stepping forward, each step bringing this being closer to your side. You sense that your guide is very close now. Such brilliant radiance. This being knows you intimately and has awaited your call. Reach out now into the mist with your hands extended toward your dream guide. As you do, be aware, feel, and experience your guide's hand gently slipping into your own. In this moment you feel a relaxation so deep that it touches the very core of your being as you are guided into the quiet realm of the night. When you go to bed each evening, imagine your guide's hand in yours. Know that this being is with you, now and forever, to guide and lead you through the mysteries of the night.

The mists now begin to clear, enabling you to see clearly the form and features of your guide. If you are not able to visualize, then get a sense or feeling of your guide. For example, you might not be able to see a waterfall, but you can get a feeling of the freshness of it. Now, take some time to be with your guide. You may wish to ask your guide's name or other questions, or you may choose simply to sit with your guide, wrapped in the gentle silence of the moonlit night.

If you desire, your dream guide will come with you night after night during your sleep to assist you in dealing with difficulties presented during the day. Your guide can also help you to gain great wisdom from the future or from the past, as well as assist you in exploring other dimensions.

Say goodbye to your guide.

At this time, you may wish to drift off to sleep. If you wish to return to wakeful consciousness, however, simply take a deep breath and, in your own time and when you are ready, allow your eyes gently to open. . . .

18.

DREAM SHIELD

A dream shield is a personal power object for the cultivation of inner power and strength. It can be used to experience deep understanding of the ancient mysteries and will keep you and your loved ones protected. The symbols that you place on your shield are rudiments of your individual mythology and will allow you to be more in alignment with your life's purpose. Following is a letter received from someone who accessed the power of a dream shield.

Dear Denise,

I wanted to let you know what happened after I took your Past Life Seminar where we did the "dream shield" technique. On Sunday night, after the seminar, I received a phone call advising me that my brother had died that morning after having a heart attack Saturday evening. I did not communicate with his widow directly because there has been lots of "stuff and junk" between us for over twenty years.

After the phone call, I talked with my good friend Gina. I commented that I probably would not attend the funeral, as I was fearful of having a family confrontation. I had a major

quarrel some years ago at my father's funeral with this brother
and his wife. Gina indicated that the funeral could possibly
be a means of deep healing for myself and that I might
not have such an opportunity for a long time. I told Gina
that I would ask for dream guidance and follow that guidance.
We continued to chat about other things and then I went
to bed.

I did not consciously create my dream shield as I turned off
the light. I recognize now, that my subconscious had already
been programmed by the dream shield process that we had done
earlier in the day at your seminar. I went to bed and slept
soundly. I woke up at 4:30 A.M. very surprised. Dream recall
is a very new process for me, as is visualization. My pillow
was sopping wet, for I had apparently been weeping. I had
a vivid dream where I was standing at the cemetery under a
canopy and I was reading a farewell letter. I felt extremely calm,
healed, and peaceful. I knew that everything was okay. I did not
have any anxiety about recalling the letter for I "knew" that I
could recall it at the office when I went to work later. Everything
felt perfect and serene.

That evening I received the details of the service and asked
Carol, my brother's widow, if I could have the time to read
my letter. My request was granted without argument even
though I could sense some attempt to manipulate me. It was
as though I was "shielded."

On Thursday, at the funeral, I read my letter and felt an
immediate sense of deep, deep peace with my brothers—both
Fred, who had just died, and my other brothers. At the end of
the reading, I placed a bouquet of rainbow-colored carnations on
the casket. After the service, as we comforted each other, there
seemed to be a feeling of deep compassion and a sense of true
togetherness. His widow thanked me for the poem and asked
me for a copy. The gathering afterward was a very warm and
friendly time for our friends and family.

It was an extremely healing process and I had a real sense

of completion. This was much more than I ever could have believed was possible.

Love,

Vi Randall

P.S. I've included the eulogy that I wrote for my brother as it was dream inspired.

EULOGY FOR FREDERIC

On November 8, 1987, the spirit of Frederic returned home. This is the fall or "earth" season, the time of dying, of gathering home all things that will nurture and sustain life through the dormant winter or "fire" season. This was Fred's season and he lived the essence well. He nurtured his family, he worked with his hands, and he enjoyed life to the fullest when in the company of his family.

Today, November 12, I honor the spirit of my brother, and I speak words of love and send him many rainbows to help him return to the Great Spirit from which all life comes. Father Sky and Mother Earth are in harmony on this day to grant him a safe journey. During the last year, his mother and older sister completed their journey and he now joins them. We will miss him as we have missed Elsia and Rondalyn, but to all things there is a season. A time to mourn. A time to cry. A time to be born. A time to die. This is our time to honor our brother, our friend, our soulmate, in our own way. This is the time for our own reflection, a time to release our fears, our jealousies, our anger, our hate and mistrust. A time to acknowledge that we are all one family on this planet earth. A time to come together, in spirit and harmony, to wish and grant each other the same love and peace that we wish Frederic. To his widow, I send understanding and love to sustain her during this transition. To his children, I send knowledge that their father taught wisdom and faith. To his brothers, strength and serenity. To all his friends and family, unconditional love.

Let each of us honor Frederic in our own way as he is laid to rest with his father. His physical journey has been completed but his spiritual journey continues. From Father Sky, I call upon the Wind to blow his spirit gently home. From Mother Earth, I call upon her to receive him home. May the spirits of Fire purify all thoughts, and may the spirit of Water cleanse and wash away his hurts, anger, and disappointments.

In closing, grant me forgiveness for my trespasses. I love you, Frederic, older brother and mentor. Thank you for being my teacher. I'll miss you.

Dream Shield Meditation

The Dream Shield Meditation is based on ancient dream techniques. This safe, easy technique is best done just before sleep. You can tape-record this meditation and play it back to yourself before bed. Speak with a very slow, relaxed voice. You might want to include a musical background. You can also read it to friends or use it with clients.

To begin the process, allow your body to assume a restful position, making sure your spine is straight. You may do this now. Good.

Now begin to take very easy, deep breaths . . . nice, easy deep breaths. Inhale and exhale. That's good. It is almost as if you are being breathed. It's as if nothing else exists except your breath. In and out. All your thoughts and cares are drifting away as you continue to breathe in and out. With each breath you take, you find yourself relaxing more and more. You find yourself moving deeper and deeper within yourself. Imagine that you are flowing into your body with the oxygen as it enters your lungs. Then, you are flowing out of your body as you exhale that oxygen. In and out, each breath taking you deeper. It is as if you are drifting and flowing with the very gentle ebb and flow of the air that you are breathing. There is a rhythm, a balance to the universe, and your breath is connecting you to that rhythm, that harmony. Breathe gently and evenly as you continue your journey into a very relaxed, yet aware, state. Allow your awareness to drift gently into your body and allow yourself to be aware of any tightness. Just notice it. Good.

If there is any tightness in your body, feel it melting away like ice on a warm summer afternoon. That's good. Now allow your imagination to begin to drift and float, and imagine you are walking along an ocean shore on a warm, softly dark, moonlit evening. Your entire body feels relaxed and you are moving with grace and ease. The soft, sensuous sounds of the ocean are serenely lulling you into a brilliant, deep, calm place within yourself. In the distance, you are aware of a great shimmering, sparkling, glimmering spot on the ocean shore. As you approach it, you see thousands of crystals lying on the sand, their luminescent beauty reflected by the light of the moon. Each crystal seems to have its own inner glow that is so magical . . . so mysterious. As you walk through the myriad crystals, each sparkles, seemingly lit by its own inner light. In the distance, you see a particular crystal . . . a special crystal that seems to draw you to it. Reach out and pick it up. The instant it touches your hand, it is as if tranquil electrical currents are flowing through your body. Take a deep breath and feel the power that is enveloping you.

As you put this dream crystal into your pocket, you begin to hear a deep, resonating tone. Touching the crystal has activated a resonance within you. Appearing before you in the moonlight is a shield. It seems translucent at first. It is only a veil of light and sound, but as you stand and observe it, it becomes solid. You are aware that carved or engraved upon its surface is a symbol—a symbol that only you can see. No one should ever know what this symbol is. It is for you alone.

Now reach forward and grasp the shield. There is security and safety afforded you just by holding this dream shield. And as you hold the shield, watch the environment begin to change.

The earth begins to shake beneath your feet. You feel mighty movements of the earth. As you walk, holding the shield, you observe the splendid scene of the earth being formed. Hills are moving and valleys forming. Mountains are pushed up into splendid jagged edges reaching for the sky. Observe as the substance of earth is moving through its creation. Earth is physical strength. It is being a part of the physical dimension. Touch your shield to the earth. Your shield has now been activated with the power of the element of earth.

As you continue walking, the winds begin to rise. The winds whip around you. Hold your shield to the wind and let the element of air empower and activate your shield. The element of air unlocks our high ideals. It is the divine process of thought.

And now the air becomes still . . . nothing is moving. Then you feel moisture, one drop, then another, then another falls. It is the beginning of the time of the Great Rains. Hold your shield over your head as torrents of rain cascade around you and your shield.

The element of water is activating your shield. Feel the strength of the element of water. Water represents intuition. It is spiritual. The power of water activates your shield.

As the rains are subsiding, great bolts of lightning punctuate the sky. Again and again, lightning streaks through the atmosphere above you, and thunder reverberates around you. Raise your shield high over your head, keeping both feet firmly planted on Mother Earth. A bolt of lightning strikes your dream shield. Energy courses through your shield, down your arms, through your veins, as the lightning grounds through your feet as your shield is activated with the power of the element of fire.

Your dream shield is complete. It has been activated by the elements of earth, air, water, and fire. You are now ready for dream exploration and dream adventures.

Now you notice that you are beside a door. Take a short time to be aware of this door. Is it big or small? Is it old or new, ornate or plain? This is the mystic door to your dreams. Take just a moment to examine it. Your dream crystal and dream shield are the keys to open this door. Decide which area you wish to explore in your dreams. Do you wish to do problem solving for a difficulty in your life? Do you want adventure and romance? Do you want to explore the psychic realm? Do you want healing for yourself and others? Decide what you want to explore in your dream realm. You may do this now. Good.

Imagine you are holding your dream crystal to your third eye area (slightly above and between your eyes). Dedicate your dream crystal to your dream quest. Hold your shield with one hand and your dream crystal in the other and lightly touch the door with your dream crystal. The door begins to open. As it does, your shield and crystal become invisible but are still a part of your energy field. You are now welcome to enter the world of dreams.

You remember to accept unconditionally whatever occurs during this dream state. If you notice your mind making judgments, just thank your mind for its concerns and keep going.

And now, step into the realm of dreams. You may do this now. Use your imagination to enhance your dreams. You may do this now.

Prepare to leave the realm of dreams. It is a realm to which you can return night after night. Begin your departure by taking a deep breath. I am going to count from one to ten, and as I do, allow yourself to begin to return to wakeful consciousness. Or, if you desire, drift off into a deep, restful sleep.

One. Every number you hear deepens your ability to remember your dreams.

Two. Your dreams are valid and you understand the meaning of your dreams.

Three. Every dream you have, whether it is remembered or not, greatly enhances your waking hours.

Four. You are feeling rested and rejuvenated.

Five. You are very rested and refreshed and your body vibrates with excellent health.

Six. Your ability to be in the right place at the right time is greatly enhanced by your dreams.

Seven. You are one of the light workers of the night and you contribute to the well-being of others during your sleep, even if you are not aware of it.

Eight. If you choose sleep, it comes soundly and easily.

Nine. You are more and more awake; more and more aware.

Ten. If you choose, you can now move to wakeful consciousness.

Sweet dreams!

19.
DREAM LOVER

*T*he dream lover meditation is designed to increase your awareness of your sensuality and sexuality. When your sexual/sensual energy is open and clear, you will naturally experience and enjoy life more fully. You can use this meditation during your waking hours or just before sleep as a means of programming your dreams for sensual encounters.

My initial attempts at creating a lover in my dreams were less than the sizzling trysts I had anticipated. My first dream lover was a pale, withdrawn, insipid lad who looked about fifteen years old (though he whiningly sought to convince me he was much older). This was definitely not what I had in mind. I terminated the dream. My endeavor the following night centered around a robust, burly man (not my type, but a definite improvement over the spindly teenager) with a noticeable bulge in his trousers. Fortunately, with my "dream X-ray eyes," I could see the oversized potato he had stuck in his trousers in the hope of luring me to his bed. I again made a hasty retreat. My next attempt was a dark, foreboding shadow of a presence who tried to force his attentions on me. Foiled again!

My fourth dream lover, finally, was a success. The dream

was set in eighteenth-century Italy. This lover was neither too young nor too old. He possessed all the correct physical equipment. He was strong, kind, and romantic. He was perfect! I even met his entire passionate Catholic family. He then informed me that we could not make love until we were married, and our marriage would not occur until after his older brother had married.

At least this last dream gave me a clue as to why I was having so many difficulties obtaining a desirable dream lover. My upbringing was making it unacceptable on a subconscious level for me to take a lover (any lover, including a dream lover), in that I was already married. In discussing the situation with my husband, David, he told me that he had always had dream lovers, and felt that they were important for his own sense of well-being. In short, he encouraged me in my nightly endeavours. So, I intensified my efforts! After a few more feeble encounters, it became *definitely* worth the effort. I strongly recommend it. One immediate benefit was that my dream escapades greatly enhanced the sexual relations I had with my husband.

Often a man or woman secretly desires to have an affair, not necessarily because he or she experiences any lack in a present relationship, but because of a desire for change or some variety. Taking a dream lover (or lots of dream lovers) is one constructive way to fulfill that desire for diversity while keeping your present relationship intact. It is also excellent for the single person, since a dream lover can appease the compulsive *need* to be with a partner. Consequently, you can be more empowered in your selection of a companion.

Preparation for Meditation

If you are using this meditation to make a tape for yourself or if you are reading to another, first create a restful setting—phone off the hook, lights low. Be in a setting where you will have little or no distraction. Use a very slow, sensuous voice when doing this meditation. If you are making a tape, you may wish to have some music in the background. Select music that you find very sensuous and arousing.

DREAM LOVER MEDITATION

To begin, make certain that your body is completely comfortable and in a relaxed position. Good. Now, check to see that your spine is straight and your arms and legs are uncrossed. That's good. As your body begins to move into very deep relaxation, notice that each breath you take allows you to move deeper and deeper within yourself. Simply watch your breath for a moment. You aren't encouraging your breath or denying your breath, just observing your breath. In and out . . . day and night . . . light and dark . . . black and white . . . male and female . . . yin and yang. There are two opposing, yet complementary, forces existing in the universe. In this moment, you are aligning and becoming one with those forces. In and out . . . Keep watching your breath. Good. Now allow each breath to become deeper and fuller . . . deeper and fuller. Nice, deep, full breaths. That's good.

Now allow your imagination to take wing and see yourself in an enchanted, moonlit meadow. The moon is spilling out of the heavens in cascading waterfalls of light. A mist of scented jasmine caresses the ferns curled up for the night. A dream owl hovers overhead, its silvery reflection in the stream below seen only by the stars. There is a quiet magic in the air.

Now spend some time imagining yourself in this secret garden of the night. Make it as real as you can. Imagine yourself using all of your senses to experience this place of quiet beauty, and see yourself walking through the meadow. If you cannot visualize, get a sense or a feeling of being in the meadow. Your body feels very graceful, very sensuous, very relaxed and easy.

You notice that in the center of the meadow there is a bed. It is a sumptuous bed. It is so luxurious and voluptuous. The pillows are soft and round and firm. Take some time to imagine this bed, making it as real as possible. Make it your perfect bed. It might be a big four-poster like your grandmother's feather bed, or perhaps a canopied bed draped with gossamer fabric lightly caressed by the warm breeze. Really imagine this bed. Now, slowly and ever so sensuously, climb into this bed. Be aware of the opulent plumpness of the pillows. Feel the silky smoothness of the sheets as you slide easily beneath the covers. It feels so good to be in this bed. Fanned by the gentle fragrance of the night, you find yourself drifting off into a deep, deep, deep sleep. Deep . . . deep . . . deep . . . sleeeeeep.

Somewhere in the magic of the night, you gently roll over and stretch. As you do, your hand brushes against a warm body. Your eyes are closed, yet you intuitively know this is your dream lover. While you tentatively explore the subtle curves in the mountains and valleys of your lover's body, you feel the faint, stirring breath of your dream lover softly in your hair. Take just a few moments to imagine the most exquisite . . . the most remarkable lovemaking. Feel your spirit, your entire being, soar.

Dawn is approaching. As you lie nestled in your lover's arms, you drift off into a contented sleep. When your eyes open, golden morning light streams through the forest trees. Your dream lover has vanished in the silent whispers of the night. A perfect rose graces your pillow.

At the end of this meditation, you can either move into sleep or return to wakeful consciousness. If you wish to return to consciousness, count from one to ten and suggest that with each number, you feel more and more awake.

DREAM MEANINGS

At the outset of our night voyage,
I am hesitant, overwhelmed
by the immensity of the crossing;
innate wisdom of my inner sage
speaks reassurances to my childlike soul—
I breathe and step out, the journey
is given when the spirit is ready.
                                        —M. Anne Sweet

20.

DREAM SYMBOLS FOR LIFE

*G*olden sunlight streamed in through my frosty morning window. I sat watching the steam rise from my cup of peppermint tea, loving the way it danced in misty swirls like ethereal sprites. Abby, my amber-colored cat, stretched lazily and curled up again, nuzzling her nose into velvet paws. Ruffling my fingers through her tawny, warm fur, I reached up and randomly flipped on the television. As I took my first sips of hot tea, I watched part of a show about a blind boy and the difficulties he encountered in life. That night, I decided to catch the late news and *coincidentally* saw the end of a show featuring a blind girl coping with her life.

The next day, as I drove home after taking my daughter to school, I passed by a bus stop. Curiously, there stood two blind men leaning nonchalantly on their white canes.

Later, driving to the grocery store, a blind man suddenly stepped out into the path of my car. I slammed on the brakes, spun the wheel, and stopped just short of hitting the frail gentleman. I pulled over to the curb to collect myself. All day I had gotten messages but I hadn't been listening.

Every day, in every way, the universe is trying to tell you something, just as your dreams are attempting to give you messages during the night. If you see a blind person in your dream, you might interpret that symbol as something you are "refusing to see" in your life. Your wakeful symbols are no less viable or significant. At the time in my life when I was being made aware of "blindness," there was something that I "wasn't seeing" regarding my life. My wakeful symbols were my higher self's way of letting me know. Unfortunately, I sometimes have to be hit over the head before I will slow down and focus on what is being communicated. When I paused and looked more closely at the symbolic experiences I was having, I confronted and released what I had been unwilling to see, or what I was being "blind" to.

Daily life is no less an illusion than dream life. In my Zen training, both wakeful and sleep images were considered illusions. We were urged to touch a deeper reality. Use the symbols that you notice in your life in the same way as you use your dream symbols. For example, just as your car may be a symbol for you and your body in your dreams, experiences relating to cars can be symbolic during your daily experiences.

One brisk September morning, Meadow, my daughter, and I were driving home from our country cabin. David had gone on ahead in our other car. Stately, tall pines caressed the low-hanging clouds as we sailed over the high mountain pass and wound our way past vacant ski slopes. Suddenly, the engine in my car began to rev uncontrollably. I laid all my weight on the brake, but my car continued gaining momentum as it raced down the steep mountain road. I grabbed the emergency brake and yanked on it frantically as I turned off the engine. Finally, my car skidded to a stop.

When I was able to get roadside assistance, the mechanic jumped out, looked over my car, and easily started it up. "There doesn't seem to be any problem with this car, lady." However, when I started the car, the engine sounded like someone had floored it. We towed the car seventy-five miles to town.

The next mechanic gave his diagnosis: "There's nothing wrong with this car, lady." Yet, when I turned on the ignition, it almost ran through the back wall of the garage. *(If you listen to the whispers, you don't have to hear the screams.)* I finally found a mechanic who determined that the cruise control was broken.

What did my runaway car represent or symbolize to me? What was I trying to tell myself? To me, a car is a symbol of my body or my physical being. (See "car" in chapter 28.) My car was racing out of control. It didn't have the ability to cruise. The only way it could operate was to get completely wound up. At that time in my life, *I* was completely wound up. I had a very intense seminar schedule and was spending most of my time thinking (or worrying) about the future instead of being in the present. My car problem was telling me to slow down and smell the flowers, to set my life's course on "cruise control" and enjoy life.

Every day, in every way, the universe is trying to tell you something. A further example of this concept is the plumbing in my house. To me, plumbing represents my emotions. If the plumbing clogs or the pipes freeze, it's usually an indication that my emotions are backing up or are frozen. If I take the time to discover what it is that I'm blocking emotionally, and allow my emotions to run freely, the pipes will generally unplug. Similarly, I have noticed that when the basement begins to flood, it is usually when my emotions are running amok and I'm not taking the time to center myself and be still.

It's also valuable to notice the little bits of conversations you hear randomly in passing. One day, as I was being led to a table in a Chinese restaurant, I heard this: *". . . don't go ahead with the project."* Upon leaving the restaurant, I turned on the radio and heard a song: *". . . don't go, baby, don't go."* On the newscast that followed: *". . . the engineers have been advised not to go ahead with the project."* Was the universe trying to warn me not to go ahead with something? I had been scheduled to go to Washington, D.C., to work on a project, but after listening to the subtle voices of the universe, I decided not to go. It was a fortunate decision. The plane I had been scheduled to take was forced to land in Chicago due to a blizzard and no planes were able to get in or out of Washington. If I had gone, I would have missed my meetings and incurred a great deal of unnecessary expense.

The people in your life can also be symbols of your inner growth. I had moved to a new city and begun my healing practice. My first client told me that she was agoraphobic. I had never heard the term before. I found that the word literally meant "fear of the marketplace" and was applied to someone who was afraid of going outside. Curiously, my next client was agoraphobic, and then, to my amazement, my third client was also agoraphobic. Three in a row!

When a symbol appears three times in my life or in my dreams, I begin to listen very carefully. I knew that I didn't fit the classic definition of agoraphobia. I was comfortable in crowds and could easily leave my home without feeling anxious. However, as I began to delve more deeply into myself, I found some raw truths. In our move, I had left behind many dear friends. My new environment seemed cold and hostile to me, and emotionally I had no desire to venture out. The agoraphobics were symbols of my not wanting to venture out into my new environment. Once I became aware of these thoughts and feelings and began to take emotional risks, not only did I begin to enjoy my new city, but I began drawing clients who were more outgoing. *Coincidentally,* my agoraphobic clients also began to get better. (See chapter 14.)

There also was a time when the majority of my clients were women who had not been able to get pregnant. Knowing that I didn't want to have any more children, I was puzzled by this symbol. But when I began to "give birth" to a new self-understanding, the women with whom I was working began to conceive, one by one.

Everything and everyone in your life, as well as in your dreams, is trying to tell you something—from the billboards you see to the formations you observe in the clouds, from simple things like losing your keys to the gifts you are given. You can use the symbols noted in this book both for dreams and for daily life.

21.

DREAM METHODS

O dreams; Keep me by you!
Let your soft-footed shadows carry me
dancing through the midnight skies,
laughing to the outer edges of the universe.

Each morning we usually wake with a light mist of memory. Elusive fragments of dreams quickly disappear and the hazy clouds clear until we realize we are here, now, awake. However, occasionally a dream is so vivid that we almost feel we could walk back into it. Sometimes these dreams continue to tug at our consciousness and we wonder what they mean for life today, or yesterday, or tomorrow.

There are many methods that you can use to interpret your dreams. Each may take you on a unique pathway in understanding yourself. How you interpret the dream is less important than the meaning that you personally derive from it. You may look at each dream as a separate and new revelation or view your dreams over time as a collective whole.

Following are some traditionally used methods of dream interpretation. You might work with several of them or use one at a time. There is no right or wrong way. Remember, have fun as you find the one that works best for you.

178

MAKE A DREAM JOURNAL

Record every dream that you remember for at least three months. Watch for recurring themes, people, places, feelings, or situations. Important messages from the unconscious can be uncovered through this method. (See chapter 6.) After you record a dream, notice any hunches or intuitive feelings. Your "gut reaction" about a dream can be a clue to its meaning.

MAKE A DREAM DICTIONARY

Make a dream dictionary containing those symbols that are unique to you. Whenever you have a dream, write down the symbols that appear. Then list the meanings that you personally assign to those symbols. Assemble your collection of dream symbols in dictionary form. Refer to this dictionary each time you dream. The more you use your dream dictionary, the more insight you will gain into your symbols. This is a powerful way to gain self-awareness.

WATCH THAT DREAM FEELING

Find the feeling or emotion that you had as a result of your dream. Now look back over your life and remember the last time you had that feeling. Recall the situation that evoked that emotion. Most often it is either that particular situation or the issues underlying it that have evoked your dream. This can be a real clue to finding the significance of your dream.

TALK WITH YOUR DREAM GUIDE

Ask your dream guide for help in understanding and interpreting your dreams. This is the method that works best for me. (See chapter 17.)

GESTALT THE DREAM

Go back into your dream and take the part of each item and each character. For example, if you dreamed about a man, a child, and a woodstove, you would say, "I am the woodstove and I represent _____." (Here you would say what wood-stoves represent to you. Perhaps they represent contained warmth or family and friends.) Next, you would say, "I am the child and I represent _____." Continue to do this for each aspect of your dream until it is clearly defined.

Now, have the different parts talk to one another. For example, put out three chairs, one representing the wood-stove, one representing the child, and one representing the man. Sit in the woodstove chair and talk to the other two chairs, saying, perhaps, "I represent family and friends and inner warmth and I think families should always be together as they are when they sit around woodstoves." Then, sit in the child chair. "I'm the child and I don't want to be with the family sitting around the woodstove. I want to be outside so I can run and play. I don't want to be tied down. I feel con-fined and stifled when I sit around with the family." Continue with this process until you have a clearer sense of the meaning of your dream.

DRAW YOUR DREAM
Draw pictures that exemplify the feelings or images that you had in your dream. Use colors that reflect the tone of the dream. It is not necessary to draw exact images. For example, a black horse in your dreams does not have to look like a horse in your drawing. You can draw the feeling of "black," "movement," or "power." This exercise can begin to free you so that some of your unconscious feelings can rise to the surface.

USE FREE ASSOCIATION
Based on Freud's most acclaimed theory, this method consists of writing associations, or the first idea that comes to mind, for each part of your dream. This may give you clues to the major themes you are dealing with in the dream. For example, imagine that you dream about a rabbit. A free asso-

ciation might be: "Rabbit—Peter Rabbit—my brother Peter who used to beat me up—hey, I'm feeling really beaten up by life these days!"

PRETEND YOU MEET A MARTIAN

Pretend that you're telling your dream to someone from another planet. The alien doesn't know anything about earth. For example, if there is a broom in your dream, how would you describe it to your friend from Mars? You might say, "A broom is a long object that you hold close to you and then push away from you. It helps you get rid of things that you don't want." After you have described the broom, examine your life to see if there is anything that you want to rid yourself of. It might be something that you are pulling toward yourself and then pushing away. As you begin to describe the parts of your dream to the alien in the most basic language, often the meaning of your dream becomes clear.

COMPLETE THE PLOT

Go back into your dream in your waking hours and rework it in such a way that *you* end up the victor. You can change any uncomfortable part of any dream. You can be the hero. Conquer your dream enemies. Make your dream have a happy ending! Visualizing an ending to your dream can help you understand its meaning.

ACT OUT YOUR DREAM

The Iroquois Indians regularly acted out their dreams in a drama. You can do this in a group or on your own. The idea is to physically act out the different aspects of the dream. This begins to integrate the meaning of your dream more deeply into your daily reality.

UTILIZE A DREAM DICTIONARY

See pages 222–321 to find the symbols that appear in your dreams. Notice which ones feel right for you. No dream dictionary will be 100 percent accurate because dream symbols are very personal, but using a dream dictionary will get you off to a good start.

USE THE ANCIENT CHINESE CLOCK METHOD
See chapter 23.

TRY THE REPLAY METHOD
Place your awareness of the dream in the right side of your brain. Play through the dream, staying in the right side of the brain. (This is the intuitive side of the brain.) Then shift your awareness to the left side of your brain. (This is the side of the brain that analyzes.) Replay your dream. Notice the difference in how your body feels when you run the dream on one side of your brain and then on the other. Notice how this elicits different emotions depending on which side of the brain you use to replay it. You may also find that your interpretation of the dream will change depending on which side you use.

22.

SEASONS

The first dream of the year;
I kept it a secret
And smiled to myself.
— Sho-u

Everything that dwells on this planet is affected by the seasons in one way or another. In ancient times, understanding the power of the seasons was considered necessary in order to understand the mysteries of life. In 250 B.C., a secret "mystery school" was founded in China that centered its teachings around the esoteric comprehension of the seasons. The teaching was preserved through secret societies of the Middle Ages and eventually blossomed into the study of astrology. Each of the seasons has a profound influence on our psyches, and each season represents an integral part of who we are. Just as we have our cycles of learning and of resting, we also have monthly and yearly cycles. Dreaming, too, follows the cycles of nature.

Winter

Under the winter moon
  The river wind
 Sharpens the rocks
        —Chora

Dreams during the winter months are the most powerful and
the clearest. They directly concern your spiritual awareness.
This is your time of inner growth, of looking within. These
dreams plant seeds for the year to come. This is the time
when visionary dreams concerning war, religion, and politics
are most likely to occur. You are more apt to remember your
dreams in winter. You are getting ready to blossom into
spring. A winter setting in a dream often indicates a drawing
inward of your energies.

Spring

  Yes, spring has come,
This morning a nameless hill
  Is shrouded in mist
          —Basho

Dreams that occur in the spring have to do with new directions. They deal with your emotional self, your feelings about
yourself and others. This is when you will most likely have
visionary dreams concerning motherhood, teachings, and disease. A spring setting in a dream generally signifies new
growth and new beginnings.

Summer

The summer moon
Is touched by the line
Of a fishing rod.
　　—Chiyo-ni

Dreams in the summer have to do with your intellectual self, your thought processes and social concerns. Visionary dreams concerning invention and science occur more during this season than any other. A summer setting in a dream can represent carefree joy.

Autumn

The autumn mountains;
　Here and there
　Smoke rising
　　—Gyodai

Dreams during autumn often have to do with completion and can concern your physical body. They have to do with sexuality, completion, and creativity. This is the time when you are most likely to get creative inspiration through your dreams. Dreaming about autumn often relates to harvest and abundance of ideas, beliefs, and material goods.

23.

ANCIENT CHINESE CLOCK DREAM INTERPRETATION

*T*he veil of fog and mystique that has surrounded Chinese medicine has begun to part in recent years, and Western doctors are beginning to give credence to this ancient art. The Chinese were stewards of a sophisticated and practical medical system thousands of years before Western doctors even began bloodletting with leeches. Magnificent finds, such as the circulation of the blood, are mentioned in the *Yellow Emperor's Book of Internal Medicine*, written more than four thousand years ago.

In Chinese cosmology, the source of all things is the tao, which is considered the law of the universe. From the tao flows the one energy. The two opposing yet complementary forces of the universe that blend to form the one are the yin and the yang. Yin represents the female energy—it corresponds to that which is dark, soft, receptive, moist, cool, and declining. Yang represents the male energy, corresponding to that which is light, dry, hot, active, and rising. It is the dance, the dynamic interaction between these two forces, that creates the life force energy of chi. Chi is the life force that exists in everything, from the most etheric matter, such as light, to the most dense, such as granite. All matter is imbued with chi, and chi is divided into different aspects as it is manifested in the universe. These different aspects or elements correspond to the different seasons, the different organs, and the different hours of the day. They all are manifest within humankind, linking us with the rest of our environment. Each hour of the day corresponds to a different organ and a corresponding emotion.

ANCIENT CHINESE CLOCK

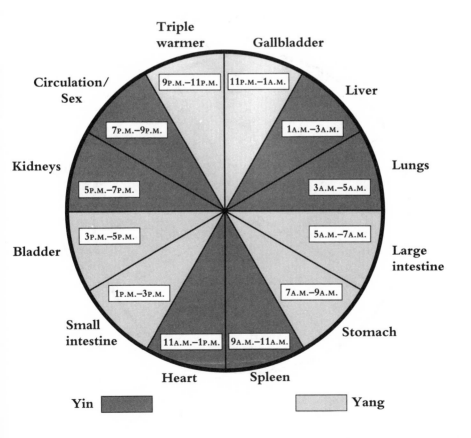

This system, based on Chinese philosophy, divides the day into different time periods. Each time period relates to a specific organ or aspect of the body. Just as each organ is thought to have corresponding emotions and characteristics, the dreams that you have during each time period are considered unique to those characteristics. Thus, it is important to note the times of your dreams in order to derive the full benefit of this method.

Listed on the following pages is an hourly guide that will help you interpret your dreams based on the times at which they occur.

11 P.M.–7 A.M.

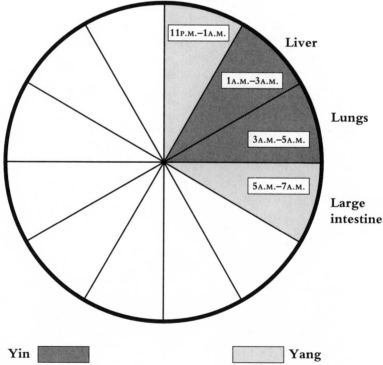

11 P.M.–1 A.M.

If you have a dream between 11 P.M. and 1 A.M., gallbladder time, your dream will likely focus around issues of unresolved anger, especially anger with regard to external circumstances. Any difficulty arising during this time period should be confronted within the dream state. This is also the time of courage. The courage you gain in your dreams will translate to courage in your daily life.

1 A.M.–3 A.M.

Dreams occurring from 1 to 3 A.M., liver time, might concern issues of self-anger, purification, and the will to live. Dreams within this time period can reveal areas that need to be cleansed or purified within your life. The liver is the one organ that can regenerate itself. Within this period your dreams will have to do with the future and with personal regeneration.

3 A.M.–5 A.M.

Dreams during the hours of 3 to 5 A.M., lung time, generally concern issues of spiritual development, inner grief, receiving love, letting go, completion, freedom, and expression. It is during this time that you are most likely to experience psychic and transformational dreams. This is also the time when you are most likely to receive dreams that are other-dimensional, or dreams from a loved one who has passed on. This is an excellent time for astral travel. The ancient Chinese said that this was the beginning of the spiritual day. You will have dreams during this time regarding new beginnings in your spiritual growth.

5 A.M.–7 A.M.

During the hours of 5 to 7 A.M., large intestine time, your dreams might concern things that are cluttering or clogging up your life. This is also a time of outer grief, discernment, caring for others, and self-empowerment. Often, it is a time to receive dreams concerning other people. In addition, dreams from the past and even past-life recall tend to occur within this time period. It is a time for processing the information and experiences that you have gathered during the day.

7 A.M.–3 P.M.

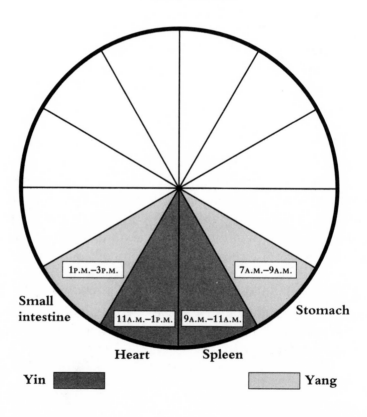

7 A.M.–9 A.M.

Dreams between 7 and 9 A.M., stomach time, tend to focus on the digestion of new ideas. They may also concern things that you can't "stomach" or assimilate in your daily life. These dreams can also deal with sympathy and empathy for others. It is a good time for the healing of others. This is also an excellent time for creative ideas to come through or to receive answers to problems that have been troubling you.

9 A.M.–11 A.M.

Dreams from 9 to 11 A.M. take place during spleen time. This is the time of self-acceptance, and dreams tend to focus on accepting the goodness of life. This is the time of healing dreams. It is the time of the mystic warrior. It is the period for the humane killing of all that isn't working in your life. This is a powerful time for physical self-healing.

11 A.M.–1 P.M.

Dreams between 11 A.M. and 1 P.M. occur in heart time. These can be dreams of joy and celebration, or they can reveal the blockages in your life. These dreams can also connect your spiritual self with your earthly self. This is another excellent time for astral travel.

1 P.M.–3 P.M.

Dreams that occur between 1 and 3 P.M., small intestine time, are for the purpose of absorbing and assimilating what you have taken in during the day.

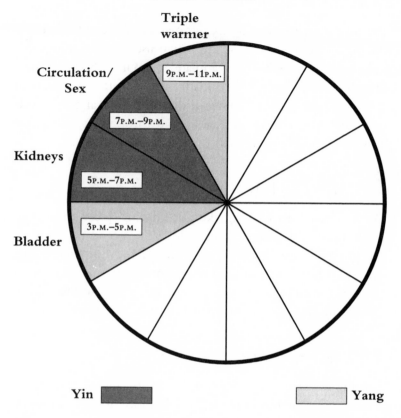

3 P.M.–11 P.M.

Triple warmer

Circulation/Sex

Kidneys

Bladder

9P.M.–11P.M.

7P.M.–9P.M.

5P.M.–7P.M.

3P.M.–5P.M.

Yin

Yang

3 P.M.–5 P.M.

Dreams during bladder time, from 3 to 5 P.M., reveal areas of fear, particularly outward fear. These dreams assist you in the release of old ideas and relationships that aren't working for you. They will help you let go and allow the power of the Great Spirit to flow through you.

5 P.M.–7 P.M.

Dreams between 5 and 7 P.M., kidney time, can assist you in letting go of inner fears. These may include the fear of being who you really are. This is the time when you will experience dreams relating to fears from your childhood. These dreams can help you resolve areas of criticism and disappointment. The kidneys are connected with the element of water, which represents transformation. This is a time of transformation through release of fear. This is also the time of the transition between death and rebirth of ideas, beliefs, and attitudes.

7 P.M.–9 P.M.

Dreams that occur from 7 to 9 P.M. are in the circulation/sex time. These tend to be dreams regarding being at the right place at the right time. They often focus on inner control issues. This is a powerful time for enlightenment dreams. It is interesting to note that within many spiritual communities, the disciples sleep during these hours.

9 P.M.–11 P.M.

If you dream between 9 and 11 P.M., known as triple warmer time, you may find dreams concerning issues of control—not so much control of yourself, but control of your environment. You also may receive dreams relating to the outer movement in your life, the breaking up of old patterns and the establishment of new ones. This is the time of establishing a balance between too little control in your life and too much control.

24.

THE MOON

She is the giver of visions. She journeys silently into the night, emissary from the land of dreams. She is the silvery white goddess, illuminator of the unconscious, revealer of mysterious forces. All tides are hers. Tides of the great seas, tides of the sky, tides of the inner realms of the night and the secret tides of death and birth . . . tides of the monthly cycles of women.

She is a celestial goddess of dreams. She carries the moon tides gently to the center of the soul . . . tides that ebb and flow. All these secrets belong to her.

She rules the great deep where all life began. She is the mistress of the inner tides that never cease, the ruler of fantasies and intuition. She is queen of the moon-washed sky, bringing creativity and vision on the dream tides of the night.

Sleep and darkness are her gentle companions. She returns month after month with renewed strength. She unites opposing elements, transforming darkness into light. She is the source of all physical and spiritual rebirth and illumination. She cascades from the doorways of heaven in waterfalls of light. She is the moon—a powerful spiritual force on our planet and ruler of the dream tides that ebb and flow in the night.

Moon consciousness, or moon awareness, arises from the deep core of our being; it is inherent to our internal instincts. To primitive people, the moon was a visible and revered symbol of our inner states of dreaming. Today, the moon touches a memory of the forgotten arts, one of which is the recall and understanding of our dreams. Ancient civilizations honored the moon because it played an important part in their everyday lives. They observed that crops grew seasonally and in tune with the cycles of the moon. Women's menstrual cycles synchronized with lunar rhythms. The moon was the ultimate symbol of fertility in the universe; her gentle light soothed dew-moistened plants after the heat of the day. The light of the moon invited life to come forth from the seeds during the night. With the same mystical force, it drew plants from the earth, the monthly bleeding from women, and tides to and from the shore. Through dreams, it was the bearer of wisdom in the night.

In past times, an important relationship was acknowledged between one's dreams and one's daily life. Since night, the special dominion of the moon, brought sleep and visions, dreams were revered as messages from the moon to be carefully followed the next day. The moon was believed to be the originator of all creativity.

Early civilizations observed that being in or out of sync with the rhythms of the moon influenced their health and balance. People measured all life by the lunar cycles. Activities from planting crops to cutting hair to engaging in battle were acknowledged to be more successful when done in alignment with the moon cycles.

Our bodily cycles are one of the most basic aspects of our existence. These internal flows seem to define the way we experience ourselves and the world around us. The moon is a significant regulator of many of these rhythms. The moon affects the tides, and even slightly distorts the earth. This cyclical pull dramatically affects our body fluids as well as our dream states. Since the body is 60 percent water, and in view of the fact that our blood has a chemistry very similar to that of sea water, it is easy to understand how our dream states and body changes synchronize with the ocean tides and the phases of the moon.

An intimate knowledge of and exposure to the moon can increase our inner knowing. Mastery of dream states can be acquired by understanding and aligning with moon cycles. All life is cyclical. Developing an awareness of moon cycles, as well as of our own life cycles, will provide us with greater insight into our dreams. To maximize our understanding and interpretation of our dreams, it is of paramount importance for each individual to create his or her alignment with the moon and its cycles.

One of the universal principles that ancient peoples learned from lunar cycles was the basic pattern for renewal. Rest, meditation, and gestation were treated with the same reverence as was productivity. The understanding of equal respect for all parts of the cycle has been most clearly retained in the Eastern concept of yin and yang and its adherence to the cosmic laws of balance.

Each cycle of the moon is divided into four smaller cycles: new moon, waxing moon, full moon, and waning moon. Each cycle lasts about seven days. There is no set moment when one cycle ends and another begins. They simply follow a flow pattern, as does our physical energy.

The new moon is the time of rebirth. During this time, rest, be still, and meditate. Dreams that occur during this time reflect the deepest and most internal movements of your inner self. This was a time when ancient Native American women sought retreat in nature in order to be still and to commune with the Creator. Amid this stillness, your dreams are preparing the soil of your inner soul for the planting of seeds in the weeks to come.

As the crescent moon appears, be aware as your energy

begins to expand. When the moon waxes, or more of it becomes visible, begin to take action in alignment with the revelations you received in your dreams during the new moon.

The full moon is the culmination of the seed planted in the new moon. During this cycle, release the fullness of your creative forces. Be alive and animated. Participate fully in life and enjoy the dance of celebration. Research indicates that this is the cycle when the most vivid dream activity occurs. The full moon is also the time when you are most likely to recall your dreams, and the number of dreams you experience also increases.

The waning moon is the time to assimilate and absorb all you have learned in the preceding weeks. Dreams during this time will be ones of reflection and introspection. When you begin to integrate your life movements with the moon's cycles, you will be flowing in harmony with the most primordial and powerful force in nature. Your dream life will become increasingly vivid and viable.

One way to integrate your life cycles with those of the moon is to create a moon ritual. In ancient moon rituals, visionary experiences occurred that were considered necessary to the balance of life, and without these states, one's understanding of the universe dwindled. It is essential to our individual and collective balance to regain an understanding of these states of being. This can be achieved by creating a moon ritual for yourself.

A moon ritual is the channeling of energies of the universe, utilizing the moon as a focal point, in order to usher yourself into more expanded levels of consciousness. All mysteries and powers of the subconscious are symbolized by moon rituals. It is that elusive quality with which the moon priestesses of old desired to merge.

A ritual can be used to change your perceptions of reality. It is a symbolic event. It can be either simple or complex in nature. The ritual attempts to make tangible an event that is occurring on an inner plane. A transformation of personality is implied in every ritual. It is a way to experience connectedness with the entire universe.

Here are some simple moon rituals that you can use to enhance your dreams.

- Stand at a window or outdoors when the moon is up during its different phases.
- Lift your arms to the moon as ancient peoples did. Feel the energy of the moon surge through you, filling every cell of your being.
- Take a moon bath, allowing rays of moonlight to bathe and cleanse you, washing over you like waves of the sea.
- Dance in the moonlight. Allow yourself to move with wild abandon.
- Leave water out in the light of the moon, then drink it just before you go to sleep.

A ritual is a stylized series of actions used to bring about change. It has its origin deep in the psyche of each individual. You already possess the ingredients within to trigger all the experiences you desire. So, create a moon ritual that speaks to your life and your needs, using symbols and artifacts that for you are representations of the inner qualities of your dreams.

The dream moon ritual I created for myself is simple. I lay out a circle of sticks or special stones. The circle represents wholeness and my dream world. Without beginning or end, it represents the source and eventual return to the source of life and unity. Within this circle I place things that are special to me and that represent the mystical world of dreams. Among these is the stone selenite, a name originating from the moon goddess Selene. This stone is an excellent tool in assisting dream recall and understanding.

To enhance the ceremonial aspect of my moon circle, I

begin by dedicating my energy to the living spirit in all things and to my dreams. I then compose a simple dream song and create a dream dance that will invoke the power of life and my own inner nature. Once I have completed my ritual, I carefully gather my treasured objects and store them in a special place until my next moon ritual.

When you first create your moon ritual and begin to participate in it, you may feel foolish or awkward. However, as you persist beyond that point, you will soon experience the sacred center. At the beginning of the ritual, your true emotions are buried under layers of linear and rational thinking. But as you persist, the right side of your brain will take over and the inner reality of the acts performed will come through. As a result, you will feel yourself in harmony with the inner cycles of nature and with your dreams and the inner wisdom of the night.

25.
COLORS

Dreaming in Color

There is no doubt that color plays an important role in almost everyone's life. Colors play a definite role in our dreams, providing us with valuable insight into the hues and shades of our life experiences.

There are several theories concerning whether we dream in color. Calvin Hall, a dream researcher who has collected records of thousands of dreams, states that two-thirds of all dreams are in black and white. He believes that only one dream in every three is colored or has color in it. Hall relates that few people dream entirely in color, and that some individuals never experience color in their dreams.[1]

This view, however, is not shared by everyone. Gladys Mayer, another dream explorer, says that all dreams are in color. She maintains that just as we all dream, yet perhaps do not remember our dreams, we all dream in color but do not recall the colors.[2]

Aldous Huxley, in his book *Heaven and Hell*, states that to be effective, dream symbols need not be in color. "It is worth remarking that, in most people's experience, the most brightly colored dreams are those of landscapes in which there is no

drama, no symbolic reference to conflict, merely the presenta-
tion to consciousness of a given nonhuman fact." He believes
that when symbols express psychological conflicts, color is not
necessary. Therefore, the color occurs in those areas without
conflict. Some dream researchers disagree with this theory,
claiming that all dreams appear to embody some type of conflict. Another disagreement with this theory is that some
people always dream in color regardless of conflict.[3]

One theory holds that the presence of color in dreams can
signify a diseased condition. One hypothesis purports that
dreams that contain a great deal of green indicate disorders of
the liver. Dreams in which red predominates warn us of the
possibility of hemorrhage or of circulation or cardiac problems. I believe that while there may be some validity to this
theory, the shade of green or red is also a factor. A forthcoming disease can be indicated by disturbing shades of colors
in dreams, but a clean spring green in a dream can signify a
major healing force, and a clear brilliant red can represent
physical strength and sexual potency.[4]

Yet another theory contends that those who dream pre-
dominantly in color are far more color conscious than the
average individual and are exceptionally talented artistically.
The proponents of this theory suggest that painting lessons
will trigger dreams in color.[5]

Knowledge of color significance in dreams is one of the
simplest yet most effective tools for understanding our dreams.
As we look about us, everything within our sight reflects
color. Where the colors change, where the shadows meet—
this defines the form and shape of everything we see. The use
of color to understand dreams has been practiced successfully
for thousands of years in most cultures that have esoteric traditions. To understand color is to understand the essence of
energy.

We are living in an expansive ocean of energy consisting of
vitally alive vibrations of different speeds and varying degrees

of intensity. This ocean of energy is a swirling dance of ever-changing matter. It is energy in the various stages of solid, liquid, and gas, each finding its temporary niche in the universe. Light and color are vibrations in this eternal play of energy. The warm colors of red, orange, and yellow have a slow vibratory rate on the electromagnetic scale, while the cooler colors of green, blue, and purple have a very fast rate.

Sir Isaac Newton, in 1666, was the first man to break sunlight into its component colors. Using a prism, Newton produced a spectrum dividing natural sunlight, or white light, into seven bands of color: red, orange, yellow, green, blue, indigo, and violet. Light is actually a vibrating, radiant energy traveling at 186,000 miles per second in the form of rays or waves. These wavelengths are measured in terms of frequency; the shorter the wavelength, the higher the frequency.

You, too, are a series of energy fields. Your entire body is constantly vibrating in fields of energy, some subtle and some manifest. You are constantly involved in movement and motion. Your body's energy fields are affected by the constantly changing energies in your environment, such as sunlight and wind, the energy fields of other people, and the energies of the food you eat. Your body—indeed, your entire being—is continuously affected very deeply by the energies of colors.

Even though we might not be consciously aware of it, we acknowledge the power of color in our lives. Our language reflects this in our expressions: I'm feeling blue today. It was a blue Monday. She's feeling in the pink. He looks at life through rose-colored glasses. He saw red. She was red with anger (or green with envy, or purple with rage). The list goes on. Color plays an important role in every area of our lives.

There was a time when color was perceived as far more significant to humanity than is currently acknowledged. In fact, it was not until relatively recently that color began to be thought of as merely decorative or entertaining. In human history as a whole, color was considered one of the most important symbols in the world. The profound meaning of each color was an integral part of all ancient civilizations that were involved in dream exploration. Mesopotamia, Egypt, Greece, China, and Tibet, as well as the traditional cultures of Native Americans and even medieval Europeans, used the power of color. Today, however, psychologists and scientists are acknowledging the use of color for therapeutic and medicinal purposes.

Researchers have discovered that certain colors trigger similar responses in people regardless of their cultural background. Orange-red is always perceived as stimulating, whereas dark blue always produces a relaxation response. It appears that color psychology cuts clear across divisions of nationality, race, and culture in a way similar to music.

Of course, you will have different shades and different hues of the seven major colors in your dreams. The clearer the color, the more accurate the meaning of the symbol. The muddier the color, the more that area is blocked for you.

Red

Red in a dream corresponds to the first chakra, the area at the base of the spine. Our drive for existence and survival is represented by red. Red stimulates the physical body to respond and act in an assertive manner. Red stimulates the heart and increases the vibratory rate. It is no accident that restaurants use red in their decor, for its stimulating effect increases the appetite. Red is also associated with sexual energy. It relates to sensations of pleasure. Red brings on reactiveness and physical excitement.

Red can also be related to anger. A clear red in a dream symbolizes clear anger. A muddy red represents suppressed anger, in the form of pugnacity, aggressiveness, sensation, tenseness, or physical strength. Our perception of time seems longer when we are exposed to red, therefore it is not an appropriate color for waiting rooms.

Red relates to direct action, active employment, will, and power. Strength, courage, steadfastness, health, vigor, sexuality, sexual love, and danger are other attributes closely associated with red. Having this color occur in a dream can be extremely vitalizing and stimulating and can assist in overcoming inertia, depression, fear, or melancholy. It is a great aid to those who are afraid of life and inclined to feel like escaping. The red ray helps us to plant our feet firmly on the earth. If you feel not grounded because you dwell on the future, having red within a dream will help root you in the present, in the "now." It supplies the energy and motivation necessary to reach and accomplish goals. Red is a "doing" color, a "get the job done" color.

Orange

Orange in a dream corresponds to the second chakra, located about three inches below the navel on most people. Orange represents our drive for social acceptance. It is a warm, stimulating color, but it is both lighter and higher in vibration than red, so the energy translates to broader fields in the body. It stimulates involvement with assisting in group and social functions, rather than concern with self-survival. Orange is a happy color. It is used by clowns the world over. It stimulates optimism, expansiveness, and emotional balance. Orange relates to the herding instinct, ambition, agitation, restlessness, exploration, and business. It can relate to pride, and to movement of the sexual energies toward the thought processes that bring about interest in politics.

People whose favorite color is orange are likely to be sensationally ambitious, competitive, expansive, optimistic, warm, and hospitable, with humanitarian instincts. They seek social

contact and acceptance. They are ambitious for their community, their nation, and their business. They like projects of
worldwide scope, and they love to expand.

Orange in a dream symbolizes optimism, confidence, change,
striving, self-motivation, enthusiasm, and courage. Orange is a
social ray. The tendency to believe too readily, without skepti-
cism or discrimination, can be healed by the orange ray. Therefore, if you tend to be suspicious or mistrusting or have selfish
pride or are even seeking power, having orange in a dream can
assist in creating balance and discrimination. The healing energies of orange in a dream stimulate our inner knowing that
we are all one. It pushes the consciousness to rise above the
self. Essentially, orange in a dream is expansive, exploratory, and
social.

Red is sensual, while orange is social. It is the drive to find
reality through other people, the drive for fellowship. The red
energy is a passion for self-preservation and self-gratification.
With orange, the drive and concern are more for social
preservation—the preservation of society, family, and social
gathering. Orange indicates being unafraid to dance and sing
and proclaim yourself as a lover of people.

Yellow

Yellow is intellectual, corresponding to the third chakra,
located at the solar plexus. It is the last of the warm, extroverted color rays. In a dream, it relates to your thinking
processes. The energy of the yellow ray stimulates your logical, linear thinking and relates to left-brain activities. Yellow
helps us to respond with mental discrimination, organization,
attention to detail, evaluation, active intelligence, discipline,
administration, praise, sincerity, and harmony. Thus, yellow
gives heightened expression and freedom, which translates
into the joy within a dream.

Those whose favorite color is yellow analyze everything,

needing always to know the "what" and "where." They require a logical framework before they can understand things. They desire originality and change and are highly creative, seeking expression in art, literature, music, and talk, talk, talk. They are flexible, expressive, eloquent, and intensely self-aware individuals who are efficient in planning and organization. The spontaneous reactions to stimuli or events unique to both red and orange energies are not experienced by stimulation by the yellow ray. Instead, there exists a more detached understanding of how the events originated—i.e., where they took place, when they will be brought to focus, and so on. Yellow understands the larger scope of life. It stimulates the need to live in an orderly world and to express our individuality and our need to understand.

The healing power of the yellow ray in a dream works on fear. Often, when you are fearful, your stomach feels queasy. Through various incarnations, a tremendous amount of fear may have been locked away in your solar plexus region, and you cannot understand the cause of your fears. Yellow in your dreams will gradually release the tension centered in your solar plexus. Yellow is very healing for judgmental, critical, verbally aggressive individuals. It stimulates flexibility and adaptability to change. When we harmonize with the yellow ray, no problem will remain unsolved under the scrutiny of our intellect. We also learn that it is better to work to change ourselves rather than others. The need for balance between our heads and our hearts remains clear.

Green

Green in a dream represents security. It corresponds to the heart chakra, the fourth energy point of the body's energy field. Green is the balance between the warm, extroverted spectrum of red, orange, and yellow, and the cool, introverted colors of blue, indigo, and violet. Thus, green stimulates feelings of love, balance, harmony, peace, brotherhood, hope, growth, and healing. I often find that my clients tend to have green in their dreams during their healing periods. People whose favorite color is green are usually generous, vital, openhearted, and nurturing. Green establishes an inner security, stimulating our need to feel secure, certain, assertive, powerful, and to love and be loved.

Green in a dream is very beneficial for any deep, brooding feelings of regret. Green is also helpful in overcoming limiting attachments. Many anxieties are created in the heart through various attachments. While it is valuable to enjoy whatever you have in the moment, it is also important to your peace of mind to develop the art of being unattached to "having."

Green is found everywhere in nature, symbolizing the abundant, replenishing forces of the universe. There will always be enough. The dollar is green and has been strong for many years. New Zealand's money used to be green, and when the color of its money changed, there was a decline in the worth of the New Zealand dollar. Green energy is also very healing for doubt and insecurity. Through meditation on the purity of green, we can call on our true, expansive, compassionate, openhearted nature. When the heart is open and we feel the love of the universe streaming through our being, we feel the greatest security and self-confidence. We learn to live without attachments and with fewer possessions. Green is a very healing color in dreams.

Blue

Blue, the first of the cool spectrum colors, is conceptual. It is associated with the throat chakra. Blue stimulates you to seek inner truth. Blue in a dream helps you to attain inner peace and emotional security and to live out your ideals. Blue stimulates spiritual security and the desire for inner understanding.

People whose favorite color is blue are apt to be idealistic, patient, enduring souls. They tend to be nostalgic, committed, devotional, peaceful, and loyal. These highly sensitive individuals have very strong commitments to their idealistic ideas and feelings. They seek contentment and peace of mind and are not prone to change.

Blue in a dream represents inspiration, creativity, spiritual understanding, faith, and devotion. The concept of time flows quickly, and memories of the past are stimulated. Blue is an ideal color for waiting rooms and places of study. If there is a lot of blue in your dream, this reflects gentleness, contentment, patience, and composure. Therefore, blue is beneficial for people who act compulsively without stopping to think. It is also extremely liberating for those who have become rigid and resistant to change. The blue ray has the power of synthesizing and combines separate elements into a complex whole. The true blue of sincerity manifests in all relationships in life. When we are sincere with ourselves, we can be sincere with others.

Purple

Purple relates to the brow chakra—intuition—and is the color most closely associated with dreams. Listen carefully to dreams that contain purple, indigo, or violet. These colors in dreams stimulate our needs to feel at one with the universe, to have conflict-free relationships, and to be in the forefront of human development. As with the color blue, the effects of these shades of purple are calming, soothing, and comforting. Very often, when one has purple in a dream, it is indicative of psychic awareness and intuition. Listen carefully to these dreams.

As we move through the color levels, it is interesting to note what happens to our concept of time. The closer we are to our senses, the more time seems to flow forward; the closer we are to our imagination, the more time seems to flow backward. When we view the color red with our senses, we receive a vision of the immediate now, like a cat eyeing a mouse. When we view the present with our intellect (yellow), we get a vision of logic, like the flow of traffic on a freeway. When we perceive with our feelings (blue), we receive a vision of history, like rings on a tree. When we view reality with our intuition (purple), we get a vision of the future, like an eagle looking down as it soars high above the plains. From that vantage point, we can see what is near but also what is beyond. Therefore, when we see purple in a dream, we are seeing beyond. These tend to be dreams of prophecy, the dreams of a visionary. A person whose favorite color is purple is usually abstract, inspired, trustful of the future, and able to tune in to the inner world of others. Purple stimulates our spiritual perspective and intuition.

White

White in a dream relates to imagination and the crown, or top, chakra. Its vibrations are the fastest and have the highest frequency in the color spectrum. Its effects on us are divine realization, humility, and creative imagination. It can be purifying, like white snow in winter. White is the color that encompasses all colors. Dreams containing white should be observed carefully. White has the energy and the power to transform the focus of the imagination. It is a useful color for those who tend to daydream or have trouble manifesting. The white and violet rays are the creative imagination leading us toward higher spiritual attunement and divine love through our dreams. People who are strongly attracted to this color have a deep sense of wonder, bliss, and self-surrender. White is also a great healing color for anyone who has negative self-image, for its energy holds the power of transformation.

RED

Inspires Freedom; determination; honor; willpower; strength; activity; alertness; independence; motivation; initiative; leadership.

Releases Anger; frustration; confusion; violence; destruction; revenge; rebellion; impulsiveness; impatience.

ORANGE

Inspires Optimism; courage; victory; confidence; enthusiasm; encouragement; attraction; abundance; kindness; expansion.

Releases Superiority; mistrust; pride; superficiality.

YELLOW

Inspires Joy; expression; ability; mental discrimination; organization; attention to detail; evaluation; active intelligence; discipline; administration.

Releases Criticism; constriction; contempt; sorrow; judgment; bitterness; cynicism.

GREEN

Inspires Encouragement; generosity; vitality; power; security; openheartedness; nurturance; self-assertion; compassion; expansion; sharing; harmony; balance.

Releases Self-doubt; possessiveness; jealousy; selfish attachment; envy; insecurity; mistrust.

BLUE

Inspires Love; wisdom; gentleness; trust; understanding; detachment; kindness; compassion; patience; forgiveness; sensitivity; contemplation.

Releases Self-pity; fear; self-rejection; separateness; isolation; worry; depression; passivity; anxiety; coldness; detachment.

PURPLE

Inspires   Inspiration; vision; farsightedness; trust in the future; tuning in to the inner worlds of others; supersensitivity.

Releases   Inability to live in the now; spacing out; forgetfulness; lack of discipline; resentment; separateness; arrogance; pride; contempt.

WHITE

Inspires   Mystical instinct; creativity; spiritual inspiration; meditation; reflection; deep inner wisdom; grace; delight; spiritual unity.

Releases   Obsessiveness; martyrdom; restriction; intolerance; daydreaminess; criticality; negativity.

26.

NUMBERS

*N*umbers play an important part in dreams. Each number has a spiritual power and significance. Through increased understanding of numbers, we gain new insight into ourselves. Essentially, numbers are only symbols. Although of themselves numbers do not cause any change, they do provide insight into our inherent potential and the energy that surrounds us. A number or series of numbers is significant if it clearly appears in your dream—for example, a number on a house, such as 723. In addition, notice the numbers ascribed to similar objects as they appear in your dreams.

Pythagoras, the Greek philosopher, metaphysician, and mathematician, took the art of divination through numbers to new heights. It was Pythagoras who first experimented with the essence of numbers, creating a science of numbers in 540 B.C. Fortunately, his teachings were not lost in the great fire that destroyed most of his library. Century after century, the secrets of Pythagoras were passed from master to student. As the student became a master, he would teach the mysteries to an initiate. This process has continued to the present day. Below are some of the metaphysical perceptions regarding numbers and what that may mean in your dreams.

ONE
Independence; new beginnings; oneness with life; unity with life; self-development; individuality; progress; creativity.

TWO
Being a couple; a balance of male/female energies; a balance of the yin and yang energies of the universe; needing people; self-surrender; putting others before yourself.

THREE
Fun; self-expression; outward giving; the Trinity—mind, body, spirit; harmony; openness.

FOUR
Self-discipline through work and service; productivity; organization; wholeness; unity.

FIVE
Feeling free; self-emancipation; active; physical; impulsive; energetic; changing; adventurous; resourceful; well traveled; curious; free soul.

SIX
Self-harmony, particularly through service by meeting responsibilities; the number of balance.

SEVEN
The inner life; inner wisdom; a mystical number symbolizing wisdom; seven chakras; the seven heavens of the Hawaiian kahunas; symbol of birth and rebirth; religious strength; sacred vows; tendency toward ritual, particularly spiritual ritual; the path of solitude.

EIGHT

Material wealth; self-power; abundance; infinity; cosmic consciousness.

NINE

The humanitarian number; selflessness; dedicating your life to others; the number of completion and endings.

TEN

Wholeness; perfection.

ELEVEN

Self-illumination; intuition; a higher expression of the energy of the number two.

TWELVE

Power within wholeness; twelve disciples; twelve planets; twelve months.

TWENTY-TWO

Self-mastery; all things are possible.

THIRTY-THREE

The inner sanctuary; the spiritual teacher; one of the master numbers of the universe.

If any numbers appear in your dream that are not listed above, here are some guidelines to assist you. Look at the individual numbers. For example, with the number 43, look at the meaning of 4, then check the meaning of 3. Or, in accordance with numerology, add the numbers together, creating the new number 7. Now look for the meaning of 7.

Another way to analyze numbers that appear in dreams is to explore the possibility that they refer to some significant

age or date in your life. The dream number may also symbolize a specific item, such as the number of children you
now have or will have, or the number of years it will take
you to reach a goal or the number of an address you had as
a child.

27.

ANIMALS

Stately grizzly bear emerges from the fog
jowls clamped around a struggling salmon;
Grandfather emerges from the study,
jaw set on determining the family destiny.
                              —M. Anne Sweet

nimals have played an important role in the evolution of mankind. To the Native American, the spirits of animals could act as guardian spirits. In most tribes, it was virtually impossible to be a medicine woman or a medicine man without seeking help from the animal kingdom. Each animal spirit represented a particular human ability or strength, and having an animal appear in a dream meant that the qualities of that animal spirit were being bestowed on the dreamer.

The coyote, traditionally, is the wise prankster and represents mischievousness. The owl can be a symbol for transformation and wisdom, and the bear can represent healing and strength. Thus, to dream of one of these animals can help you embrace its qualities in your life. Children, and individuals who are close to nature, tend to dream of animals considerably more than most adults. When a person begins to align

216

with the cycles of nature, animals will play a greater role in his dreams, and he will begin to assimilate the associated qualities. In some shamanistic practices, when one dreams of the same animal three times, it signifies one's power animal. A shaman can have many power animals, or totems, but more often than not he will have one main totem. An animal appearing in your dreams may be your totem; it may also represent the qualities associated with that animal.

Calling Animals

As you begin to enter the animal kingdom through your dreams, you will begin to find a deeper connection with the animal kingdom in your waking life.

The Native American heritage was closely interwoven with the animal kingdom. Indians developed the skill of "calling" animals as a necessity for survival. They learned to speak with the elk, deer, and buffalo spirits, asking for guidance in regard to the hunt. There was reverence involved in any taking of life. It was believed that the spirit of the animal evolved through sacrificing itself to provide sustenance for the tribe.

The ability to call animals leads to a deepening of your connection with the earth's cycles. I have discovered that even those who are certain that they cannot master the calling technique are able to do so once they connect with the animal kingdom in their dreams. This practice has definitely helped me in reaffirming my connection to Mother Earth.

I recall an incident in Mexico. It was 4 A.M. and I was resting quietly on a dark beach in a small fishing village north of Puerto Vallarta. I hugged my knees close to my chest and felt the deep rhythm of the gentle ocean. As I watched a lone seagull silhouetted against the velvet predawn sky, I found myself wondering about life's purpose. I generally do not think of such things, as I don't believe in a random universe, yet in that early morning solitude I was wrestling with questions about God and the meaning of my life. Each ocean wave seemed to echo my hollow thoughts.

As night receded and the soft blanket of darkness melted into vivid blue and violet, I walked slowly back to the bungalow I shared with my family. I was greeted by my husband, David. He was on his way out to go fishing with a local fisherman. I had never before fished in the ocean, but I thought it might ease my questioning heart, so I decided to accompany him.

As we glided swiftly through the calm waters, I allowed my consciousness to penetrate deeply into the azure ocean, hoping to connect with the spirit of the sea. For many years I have had the ability to call animals, due perhaps to my Native American heritage. When I call animals I generally bond with the spirit of one particular species of animal at any given time. However, that morning, I simply wanted to connect to the entire spirit of the sea. Although my earlier mood had left me doubting my ability to connect with any spirit at all, I asked to experience some of the wonders of the sea. I did not have any particular species in mind.

Suddenly, with the power of a charging locomotive, forty feet of raw energy shot up from the sea like a giant missile, leaving a shimmering geyser of ocean spray. Again and again, whales surged up through space, leaving a fountain of spray and foam.

Then, just as suddenly, there was silence . . . the deep, still silence of a fourteen-foot boat rocking gently on a calm sea. The majesty of those moments of power and grace held us stunned. Then, piercing the silence, within feet of our small boat, a younger whale arced out of the depths and seemed to hang in the air. Rivulets of sparkling water streamed down its sides and back into the ocean foam. Just as serenely as it had appeared, it was gone. Silence . . . stillness . . . awe.

The old fisherman was overwhelmed. Although he had

been out on the water nearly every day during the last six fishing seasons, he had never seen anything like that morning's display. We three sat quietly, pondering what we had witnessed.

"Sharks!" David said urgently, shattering the mood.

As our eyes followed the ominous black fins, there was a sudden burst of joy dancing skyward from the sea. Dolphins were playfully dipping in and out of the water near us. The fins belonged to dolphins, not sharks.

There were at least fifty dolphins near the boat, so near that I could reach out to within inches of some of them. The fisherman, unnerved by so many of them near his boat, turned up the engine and tried to speed away. No matter how fast the little boat went the dolphins kept up with us! Finally, the pod began to trail off, but two of them remained nearby, perhaps to keep us company. As we slowed our speed, the pod kept its distance. We watched the sun dance in reflections off their backs until they blended into the blue of the distance. The very confused fisherman could only mumble something about "mating season."

This unforgettable connection with the animal kingdom reaffirmed how much I was a part of all things.

How to Call Animals

Learning to call animals helps you to enter into the unseen realms and also assists you in entering into the unseen realms of your dreams with comfort and courage.

First step. Embrace the reality that you can indeed connect deeply with plant and animal spirits.

Second step. Begin to program your dreams to connect with the animal kingdom.

Third step. Reach out in your imagination to the spirit of a particular animal or plant. If you are trout fishing, you might imagine what the trout spirit would be like. Then, converse with that spirit just as you would with a friend.

"Greetings, Trout Spirit! I come to you in dedication to and love of the trout kingdom. I ask that you send forth one of your members in dedication. We know there is no death . . . only transformation . . . and as one of your species comes forth, we accept the gift as a great service, and you will be honored."

At about that time, expect a tug on your line.

Fourth step. Each animal and plant has its own sound or vibration. Imagine what the sound is, then attempt to duplicate it vocally. If you have difficulty with this, imagine that you hear the sound in your mind, or imagine that you are making the sound. This is the "call." Remember not to doubt yourself or your ability to do this. Doubt is the greatest barrier to success with this technique.

You can also practice the call just before sleep. Call for a particular animal to come in your dreams, then listen carefully to the message given in each dream.

My calling has sometimes backfired. Once, when I noticed a swarm of bees in the neighborhood, I impulsively decided it would be wonderful if the bees could hive in our backyard so that my daughter could watch them through the window. I had never attempted to call anything in the insect world, but I imagined it wouldn't be that different from calling a plant or an animal.

First, I tried to find the vibration, tone, or resonating quality of the bee kingdom. Once I had a sense of the tone, I repeated it mentally. I sent out the call and waited. Nothing happened.

About an hour later, I heard my daughter screaming. I ran outside—to be greeted by a huge swarm of *wasps*! They were settling in to make our backyard their new home.

28.

DREAM SYMBOLS DICTIONARY

*It is the dreamer himself
who should tell us what his
dream means.*
    —Sigmund Freud

ny dream dictionary can instill a false sense of security in the interpreter and stop any further search for understanding. For example, Freud's view of cylindrical objects as phallic symbols may direct the dreamer into a particular frame of mind. It is interesting to note that people who are seeing a Freudian therapist tend to have Freudian dreams, while those working with a Jungian therapist tend to have Jungian dreams. Patients of humanistic psychologists have a predominance of humanistic-type dreams. Those involved with psychic phenomena tend to have psychic dreams. Our belief systems seem to program the content of our dreams.

Dream authorities don't often agree on what dream symbols mean. The use of a dream dictionary is, at best, a vehicle to help you find your *own* interpretations. Since authorities in the field cannot agree on definitions, it is wise to remember that only the dreamer can know the true meaning of a dream.

For example, a dream that contains green apples could be interpreted many ways. One dream dictionary claims that green apples indicate a loss through one's own foolishness. Another might suggest an upset stomach. Still another might associate the apple with the Garden of Eden and point out the aspect of temptation. However, for you, green apples may relate to your visits to your grandfather's orchards. Perhaps your grandfather took you along as he walked among the trees and you were able to share his pride and pleasure as he saw the results of his hard work. Your memories may include a variety of feelings, from the love you felt for your grandfather to the anxiety associated with the hard work necessary to bring forth the harvest. Your dream may relate to these feelings.

Sometimes you will find that the symbol is a metaphor. The pine tree in your dream that kept appearing in the strangest places may have to do with something you are longing or "pining" for. The panting dog that seems to be so "hot" may be a residual childhood memory of eating a ball park "hot dog" with your dad.

Remember, only the dreamer, not the interpreter or a list of meanings, can know the true meaning of his or her dream. So, use the suggestions in this book only as a place to start interpreting your dreams. Some of these dream meanings are literal, some are common symbolic interpretations, some are metaphors or puns, and some are just plain intuition. (For more in-depth symbol definitions see Denise's book *The Secret Language of Signs*, Ballantine.)

After you have had a dream, read over the following dream meanings and symbols to see if any seem to fit. Find out what meanings you assign to that symbol. Rather than being a definitive guide, the meanings listed here are to stimulate *your* inner knowingness.

ABANDONED
Feeling left out or not included.

Leaving behind people, circumstances, or characteristics that aren't necessary anymore.
Need for self-acceptance.

ABDOMEN
Often represents the second chakra. (This energy center, located in the area beneath the navel, is associated with emotions.)
Vulnerability.

ABDUCTION
Feeling out of control or that you have no control in a situation.

ABORIGINE
The primordial part of you; your instinctual self.
Part of your basic nature that may still be foreign to you.

ABORTION
Fear of loss of new birth within yourself.
Miscarriage of justice.

ABOVE
Inspiration; the higher self.
Things looming above you; fears that seem bigger than you are.

ABYSS
Bringing to consciousness a fear that has long been buried.

ACCIDENT
Going too fast in life; a need to slow down and integrate.

ACE
Hidden talents; an ace up your sleeve.
Excelling at something.

ACHILLES TENDON
A place of vulnerability.

ACORN
Great self-potential.

ACTOR/ACTRESS
The roles we play in life are only illusions.
Deception; false appearances.

ADDICT
Giving away power to someone or something.

ADOLESCENT
Great change.
Gathering power for new beginning.

ADRENALS
Anxiety; an adrenal rush.

ADULTERY
Conflict between duties and desires.
Being drawn to a quality in another that you feel you lack.

AIRPLANE
High ideals.
Soaring to new heights.

ALCOHOL
Dulling the senses; not feeling.
May symbolize camaraderie; wine, women, and song.
May relate to transformation. (Jesus said, "This is my blood,"
    in reference to the Last Supper.)

ALIEN
A part of yourself you aren't acknowledging.
Going home.
May represent higher wisdom.

ALLIGATOR
Hidden, formidable strength and power.
Trouble below the surface.

AMPUTATION
Giving up that part of yourself associated with the limb in the
    dream. (An amputated leg may mean you feel you don't
    have a leg to stand on; a hand may signify inability to grasp
    a situation.)
Releasing parts of yourself that you thought were integral to
    your identity but that aren't really a part of your true being.

ANCHOR
Strength; being grounded.
Attachment to a person or place.

ANGEL
A spiritual messenger; our most divine ideals. (Many prophets'
    visions are based on the appearance of an angel in a dream.)
Listen carefully to what is being said.

ANKH
Ancient Egyptian symbol of spiritual wisdom.

ANKLES
Mobility.

ANT
Industrious; productive.
Community or social cooperation.

ANTENNA
Transmitting and receiving ideas and energy.
Awareness of the world around you; tuning in.

ANTIQUE
A connection with the past.
An old pattern or belief system that is no longer useful.

ANTLERS
Protection of the divine masculine part of yourself.

APE
Primitive power.
Mischief maker.
Copying; imitating.

APPLAUSE
Self-acknowledgment; needing acknowledgment from others.

APPLE
Wisdom.
Healing potential.
Wholeness.

ARCHERY
Specific direction; clarity; single-mindedness.
Pointing to one specific thing.

ARGUMENT
Parts of yourself are in conflict.

ARK
Safety and protection amid the waters of emotion.

ARMS
Reaching out.

ARMY
Major obstacles to be overcome.
Opposition.

ARROW
Clear direction; a goal; a straight course.

ARTIST
Creative expression in life.
Potential artistic ability.

ASHES
Spiritual purification.
The transitory nature of life.
Sorrow and humiliation.
In some cultures they have a purifying power.

ASTHMA
Inability to get enough oxygen may indicate suppressed grief.
Going too fast; not being able to catch your breath.
Stress; not feeling connected with life.

ASTRONOMER
Looking ahead.
Highest ambition.

ATOMIC ENERGY
Incredible energy potential; a need to harness that power.
Tuning in to the collective-conscious fear for global and personal safety.
Kundalini fire awakening within; great potential for spiritual expansion.

ATTIC
High ideals. (The top floor represents the upper chakras.)

AUDIENCE
Congratulations!
The audience responds positively: an acknowledgment of self-acceptance.
The audience responds negatively: you need to work on self-acceptance.

AUNT
The industrious part of yourself (ant).
May refer to your aunts.

AURA
Bright and clear: clarity and good health.
Dim and close to the body: lack of clarity; health disturbances.

AWAKE
If you are awake and aware during a dream, this is probably a lucid dream.
See chapter 9.

AX
Fear of loss.
Wielding power with certainty.
Cutting away that which is not needed.

BABOON
Community-minded; social.
Oafishness.

BABY
A new birth within yourself.

A positive outcome for the future.
Birth of a new idea.

BACK
Support, strength.
Retreat, back up.

BADGER
Baiting or teasing.

BAGGAGE
Unnecessary things or thoughts that you carry around.

BALL
Completion; wholeness; unity.
A social occasion; suggests joy.
Can have sexual connotations.

BALLOON
Unrestrained joy.
Soaring to new personal heights.
If the balloon breaks, an illusion is shattered.

BASEMENT
The base or root of a problem.
Your physical energy. (Very often a house will represent your
    body, with the attic associated with upper chakras and the
    basement with the lower chakras.)
May indicate the subconscious.

BAT
Fear of the unknown.
"Batting" around an idea.

BATHING
Purification.
Washing your hands of a situation.
Baptism or rebirth.

BATTLEFIELD
Deep inner conflict. (The antagonists are either those to
    whom you feel hostile in waking life or are symbolic of
    inner conflict. Remember, every person in your dream is
    most often an aspect of yourself.)

BEACH
The border between the subconscious, emotional part of you,
    represented by water, and the earthly, physical side of you.
Balance.
Purification; rejuvenation.

BEAR
Mother Earth.
The protective, mothering, female aspect.
Force and power.
Cuddly; lovable.

BEAVER
Busy; industrious.
Prosperity through your own efforts.

BED
Sexuality and intimacy.
Comfort; security; eternal womb.
Rejuvenation; nurturance.

BEDBUG
Something unpleasant that is covered up.
Small nuisance.

BEE
Busy; industrious.
Social cooperation.
The possibility of hidden sweetness.
Feeling "stung" by some circumstance or remark.

BEETLE
Represented eternal life to the ancient Egyptians.
May indicate good luck.

BELL
If the sound is clear: a resonance within the wellspring of life.
A warning.
Joyous developments.

BILL
Karmic payment.

BIRD
Soaring to new heights; soaring above your problems.
Omen of good fortune.
If singing, may be the harbinger of good news.

BIRDS' EGGS
New beginnings.
In a nest, can signify money.

BIRTHDAY
New beginning.

BLADDER
Fear of letting go; holding on to old beliefs and attitudes.

BLIZZARD
Emotional upheaval.
A "snow job" on someone or on you.

BLOOD
Life force; nourishment; power; energy.
Psychic energy.
If you were bleeding: an energy drain for you.

BOAR
Someone or something is boring.
A swinish personality.

BOAT
Traveling through emotional times. (The water symbolizes your emotions, and the boat represents you and how you are handling your emotions.)

BOIL
A situation about to erupt.
Suppressed anger.

BOTTLE
Feeling bottled up.
Notice the size and color of the bottle and whether the cap is on or off. A clean bottle signifies more clarity in your life than a cloudy one. A bottle with the cap off is more "open" than one with the top securely fastened.
A message in a bottle can be an answer from an unexpected source.

BREAD
Communion with others.
Abundance.

BRIDE/BRIDEGROOM
The peak of the feminine force within us.
New beginning.

BRIDGE
Connection between one realm and another.

BROTHER
The religious male aspect of the self.
Common tie; brotherhood.

BUFFALO
Abundance; harvest; plenty.
Sacred to the Native American.

BUG
Small annoyance.
Inconvenience.

BULL
Great strength; force; power.
Optimistic sign.

BULLDOG
Tenacity; holding power.
Defiance.
Seize the opportunity and don't let go.

BURIAL
Death of old patterns and thought forms.
Denial of a situation.

BUTTERFLY
New beginning on a higher plane.
Rebirth; inner beauty; transformation.
Romance and joy; social success.
Gentle enjoyment.

BUZZARD
Feeling picked on or preyed upon; preying on others.
Contemptible; rapacious.

CABIN
In the woods: peace and contentment.
On a boat: see "Boat."

CACTUS
A prickly situation.
Something or someone that can't be touched.

CAGE
Self-imprisonment through fear.
Feeling trapped.

CALF
Happy, carefree youth in healthy surroundings.
May refer to the calf of the leg.

CAMEL
The ship of the desert; a way to get through a difficulty.
Endurance.

CAMERA
Keeping a distance between yourself and life.
Preserving the past; preserving fond memories.

CANAL
Childbirth.
A directed and narrow emotional path.

CANARY
Music; harmony.
May indicate tattling or telling of secrets.

CANCER
Something is eating away at you emotionally.

CANDLE
Your spiritual life force; your true inner light.

CAR
Your physical body or yourself.
Notice where the car is going, the condition of the car, and
    who is in it.

CARDS
The game of life; your destiny.

CARPENTER
Making repairs in your life.
Rebuilding physically, emotionally, and spiritually. (Jesus was
    a carpenter.)

CAT
The intuitive self.
The feminine essence or female part of yourself. The goddess
    within.

CATERPILLAR
Unharnessed potential of which you are unaware.

CAVE
A powerful symbol.
Your great spiritual wealth; your unconscious self.
Consolidating your energy.
Feminine principle; womb of the Mother Earth.

CEMETERY
Rest; peace.
Fear of death.

CHAIN
Many together, creating strength.
Feeling "chained" to a situation.

CHAIR
Your position or attitude; where you "sit" in regard to the
matter.
Rocking in a rocking chair may indicate an out-of-body
experience or a building of psychic energy.

CHAMELEON
Adaptability; flexibility.
Whimsy.
Capricious; changing.
Not showing one's "true colors."

CHICKEN
Cowardice; timidity.
Counting on something prematurely.

CHILDREN
The child within you; those inner aspects of yourself such as
playfulness, joy, openness.
The child part of you isn't being acknowledged.

CHRIST
The God force within you.
Love.
Sacrifice.

CHURCH
Faith; hope; love.
The temple of the soul.
Sanctuary; haven; safety.

CIRCLE
A very powerful universal symbol.
Harmony; beauty; balance.
Completeness; totality; wholeness.

CLAM
Someone is not talking; lack of communication.
Concern over something that must be kept secret.

CLIMBING
Going up; personal ascension toward a business or a
   personal goal; reaching the top of the ladder in your
   profession.
May have sexual connotations; sexual excitement.
In Jacob's dream, he climbed to heaven.
Climbing down can mean the opposite of ascending; the
   exploration of your subconscious.

CLOTHES
Your outer persona.
The roles that you play in life.

CLOUDS
A positive, healthy sign.
Clear clouds: spiritual uplifting; inner peace.
Storm clouds: spiritual questioning; a personal storm is
   brewing.

COBRA
The power of the kundalini energy.

COCK
Strutting; proud; egotistical.
Masculine energy.
About to erupt or go off, as when a gun is cocked.

COCKATOO
Showy.
Talking without thinking.

COLON
Elimination of things from the past.

COLORS
See chapter 25.

COMET
Heralds tremendous personal and spiritual expansion.
A powerful symbol.

COOK
Nourishment.
Material comfort.

COOKING
Synthesizing the ingredients in your life.
See "Cook."

CRICKET
Joy.
Domestic happiness; peace at home.
Long life.

CROCODILE
Dishonesty; a show of false feeling as in "crocodile tears."
Hypocrisy; it's a "crock."
Trouble beneath the surface.

CROSS
A universal symbol of infinite balance and wholeness from the
    most remote times.
Jesus; Christianity.

CROWD
Anonymity; secrecy.
Strangers or something strange.
Your perception of the crowd's opinion of you is your sub-
conscious opinion of yourself.
Feeling a part of something larger than yourself.

CRYING
Emotional release of something still in the subconscious
during daily reality.
Joy from resolving a difficulty or releasing an attitude that was
not serving you.

CRYSTAL
Spiritual transmitter and magnifier.
A powerful symbol of clarity and spiritual energy; the symbol
of the mystic. Listen carefully to this dream.
See chapter 7.

CUTTING
Depending on the context, can refer to the cutting away of
undesired opinions, habits, attitudes, and beliefs.
If you are cut and bleeding, you are losing your vital force.

DAM
Pent-up emotions about to release.

DANCING
Joy; the dance of life.
Sexual enthusiasm; wholeheartedness.

DARK
The unknown; your subconscious.
Your fears.

DAUGHTER
The female-child part of you; may be your daughter.
Eternal youth.

DAWN
A new awakening.

DEATH/DYING
Not a bad omen.
Transformation; the death of old patterns and programs; making way for rebirth.
Very rarely indicates the death of one who is dead in your dream.
Usually indicates the death of an old belief system of yours, represented by the dying person.

DEMON
See "Devil."

DESERT
Jesus went to the desert for spiritual rejuvenation.
Desolate; forsaken; barren; no growth.

DEVIL
The internal struggle between the part of you that you consider "good" and that part you consider "bad."
Fear.

DIRT
Grounding; connection with Mother Earth.
Something in your life needs to be cleaned up.

DISEASE
Disharmony; dis-ease.

DOG
Faithfulness; loyalty.
Protection; rescue.
Friendship.

DOLPHIN
Unharnessed joy; playfulness; spontaneity.
Intelligence.
Spiritual enlightenment.
A significant dream symbol.

DONKEY
Patience.
Stubbornness.

DOOR
Great opportunity for new adventure and self-discovery.
Open door: you are ready; closed door: it is not quite time.
Significant symbol.

DOVE
Peace; freedom.
Someone or something with which you wish to make peace.

DRAGON
A powerful symbol.
Life force; great potency.
Dragon fire is very purifying.
"Slaying the dragon" is confronting and overcoming fear.

DREAM
If you dream that you are having a dream, you are most likely
   lucid dreaming.
See chapter 9.

DROWNING
Feeling overwhelmed by emotions.

DUCK
Get out of the way of something.

EAGLE
Very significant to the Native American.
National power.
Your spiritual, soaring self.
The ability or need to be farseeing.

EARS
Being willing to hear the truth.

EARTH
Mother Earth.
The female, receptive, rejuvenating principle of the universe;
    womb; sensuality.

EARTHQUAKE
Great change approaching.
Fear of the change you are undergoing.

EGG
Wholeness.
New life; new potential.
A powerful symbol.

ELECTRICITY
The bioelectrical systems that surge through you; the life
    force.

ELEPHANT
Something that needs to be remembered.

Thick-skinned.
Ponderous, powerful, and wise.

ELEVATOR
See "Climbing."

ELF
See "Fairy."

ELK
A reassuring sign.
Power; beauty; dignity.
The power to overcome obstacles.

ESCALATOR
See "Climbing."

EXPLOSION
Personal crisis, particularly in regard to a relationship.

EYES
Being willing to see; clarity.
I; myself.

FACES
An unknown face or faces may represent those parts of your-
    self that you aren't currently experiencing.

FAIRY
A spirit of nature.
Bringing to manifestation your inner desires.

FALLING
Loss of control; feeling out of control.
In the process of learning to walk, we often fall. If you are on

unsure ground in a situation or are experiencing a personal growth spurt and are unsure of yourself, you will likely dream of falling.

FAT
Suppression of emotions and feelings.
Abundance.

FATHER
The Divine Father; God.
Protector; provider.
May refer to your father or father image.

FEAR
If you are fearful of anything in your dreams, face it. It is most likely an unacknowledged part of yourself. (Imagine going back into your dream and facing the fear.)

FEATHER
An excellent dream symbol.
Connection to the heavens and the Creator.

FEET
Putting your best foot forward; understanding.
Connection with the earth.
Grounding.
Being afraid or unwilling to step forward.
Having the courage to step forward; movement.

FEMALE
The feminine energy; the female within.
The receptive energy; yin.

FIGHTING
Suppressed emotions; the need to have and enjoy all of your emotions.

FINGERS

The details of life.

Pointing a finger at something or someone.

Little finger: manipulation; being wrapped or wrapping around the little finger.

Ring finger: union; marriage.

Middle finger: sexuality.

Thumb: will; thumbs up: go ahead; thumbs down: forget it!

FIRE

Kundalini life force within you.

Potency; psychic energy.

Opening to spiritual communication and energy.

Initiation.

Sexual passion.

Purification by fire.

FISH

Spiritual food.

A symbol of Christianity.

May be a desire for acknowledgment or compliments.

Misrepresentation; something seems "fishy."

FLAME

Your eternal bright flame.

The light of Spirit.

See "Fire."

FLOATING

You are in harmony with your intuition and your emotions; great spiritual alignment as you move toward feeling at one with all things.

FLOOD

Overwhelming emotions.

FLOOR
Your foundation or your support.

FLOWERS
A happy omen of beauty and unfoldment.

FLYING
Flying through the air: astral travel. (See chapter 13.)
Moving beyond the bounds of physical limitation.
A very significant sign.

FOG
An obstacle.
An area of your life that you can't see clearly.

FOOD
Nourishment: can be spiritual, mental, physical, or emotional.

FOREST
Abundance; growth; strength.
Protection.
Feeling overwhelmed; you can't see the "forest" for the trees.

FORK
A fork in the road may mean you will have to make a decision.

FOUNTAIN
Spiritual rejuvenation.
Excellent sign of intuition.
Spiritual wellspring.
Listen to what you are being told.

FOX
Slyness; sneakiness; manipulation.
May indicate physical attraction.

FROG
The beauty behind surface ugliness.
Inconsistency; hopping from one thing to another.

FROZEN
Emotionally closed off.

FRUIT
Reaping the rewards of your labor.
A fruitful harvest; bearing fruit.

GALAXY
Unlimited possibilities.

GALLBLADDER
Anger; he had a lot of gall.

GARBAGE
Things you no longer need in your life.
Things you need to release.

GARDEN
Creative activity.
Peace.
If the garden is well tended: harvesting the results of your labor.
If the garden has weeds: there are things in your life that you
   need to weed out.

GENITALS
Potency; power; sexuality.
Impotence.

GHOST
Some part of your feelings about a particular person have not
   solidified.

May be undelivered communication from someone who has died.

GIFT
Acknowledgment of the growth you have made.
Good news is coming.

GIRAFFE
Stretching for what you want.
Someone above the crowd.
Stiff-necked or unbending.

GLACIER
Frozen emotions.

GLIDER
If you are soaring in a glider, you may be having an out-of-body experience. (See chapter 13.)
Riding on the winds of change in life; going with the flow.

GOAT
Lecherous; old and cranky.
Feeling blamed or made the scapegoat for something you haven't done.

GOD/GODDESS
Incredible unity and oneness; universal love; total self-acceptance in the moment.
Power to create and manifest.
A most powerful symbol.

GOLD
Great inner treasure.
The golden light of inner peace.
Heart of gold.

GOOSE
A prod in the rear; you want someone or something to get going.
Acting foolishly.

GRANDFATHER
The wise old man; the mature aspect of yourself; the part of you that knows.
May refer to your own grandfather.

GRANDMOTHER
The wise old woman; the mature aspect of yourself.
May refer to your own grandmother.

GRASSHOPPER
Living for the moment with disregard for the future.

GRAVE
Serious.
Self-imposed limitations; making your own grave.

GREYHOUND
Speed; swiftness.

GURU
Guidance; the guru within.
Listen to this dream.

HAIR
If brushing your hair, you are getting the tangles out of a situation.
Cutting your hair may signify new beginnings.
Braiding your hair may indicate forging new links.
Putting gel or mousse on your hair may mean smoothing out a situation.

Hair falling out may mean that you are worried.

Thick, luxurious hair indicates good health.

Energy streams out of the crown chakra, at the top of the head. Thick hair can symbolize great spiritual power flowing out of this energy center to connect you to Spirit.

HALO

A blessing.

HANDS

Negative: can't get a handle on it; can't handle it; can't grasp it.

Backhanded compliment.

Positive: I can handle it.

HATRED

An emotion that you aren't fully allowing yourself to experience in waking life.

Hatred in dreams helps to release that emotion so it doesn't damage you physically or emotionally.

Often, hatred in dreams is not directed toward the person or object seemingly hated; it generally reflects self-anger, and the person or thing represents the part of yourself with which you are angry.

HEAD

Getting ahead; headway; thinking; analyzing.

HEART

Love; bliss.

The center of being.

HEAT

Passion; intensity.

Desires can be awakened by the stirring of the kundalini fire.
Anger.

HEAVEN
Enlightenment; bliss; oneness; peace.

HEELS
He was a real heel.
To heel or be commanded to walk in a certain way.

HELL
Personal difficulties in your life.

HEN
Domestic, nesting instinct.
Plump; satisfied.

HIPPOPOTAMUS
Weighty; ponderous.
In ancient Egypt, the goddess Taueret, who attended all
    births.

HIPS
Positive: support; power; throwing your hip into it.
Negative: fear of moving forward.

HOG
Overindulgence.
Feeling that you are not getting or are not giving your
    share.
Selfishness.

HOLE
Something that you are not acknowledging or facing.
A "hole" in your argument.

HOME/HOUSE

Approximately one-third of all dreams take place inside a building, usually a house or home. The most common association for this is one's physical self or spiritual self, or both.

Whatever is happening to the house is what you are experiencing happening to you. For example, if the plumbing is clogged, it may be that your emotions (symbolized by the water in the pipes) are blocked.

The different rooms in the house symbolize different aspects of oneself.

Kitchen: nourishment; sustenance; creativity as in "cooking" up ideas.

Hallway: a transition area.

Bathroom: elimination of the old.

Basement: your subconscious

Attic: high ideals and aspirations.

Waking in a dark room represents exploring unknown parts of ourselves.

Clutter in the house indicates areas of our lives that we need to clean up or things that we need to discard. (Note which room is cluttered.)

HORSE

Expanded sense of self.

Freedom; movement.

Questioning another's motives; "Don't look a gift horse in the mouth."

HOSPITAL

Center of healing.

HYENA

Noisy; merriment not appropriate to the situation.

ICE
Frozen emotions.
To be on thin ice refers to a dubious circumstance.
Slipping on ice means being in a circumstance where you
    don't feel on stable ground or are unsure of yourself.

ICEBERG
The tip of the iceberg signals blocked emotions beginning to
    surface.
Drifting without emotional direction.

ICICLES
Whatever emotions have been blocked are beginning to
    release; there will be much more flow in your life.

ILLNESS
Can indicate that your body needs attention.

IMPOTENCE
Insecurity; fear.

INCEST
Integrating parts of yourself; integrating the adult part of you
    with the child part, or the male part of you with the female
    part. Remember, most often the different people in a
    dream are different aspects of yourself.
Can refer to very deep unsolved issues from your life.

INDIAN
A deep, primordial connection to nature.
A part of your basic nature that is still foreign to you.
Higher self-guidance.

INITIATION
Awakening to a new level of consciousness.

INJURY
See "Illness."

INSECT
Something is bugging you.
Maggots represent decay; butterflies are transformational; flies
   are small annoyances; ants are industrious.

IRON
Pressing out problems.
Too many irons in the fire.

ISLAND
Self-contained.
No man is an island.
Refuge.

IVORY
Favorable sign for all concerns.
Purity; strength.

IVY
Stability; wealth.
Clinging; dependence; attachment.

JACK
Diversification; jack-of-all-trades.
A car jack may indicate the relief of a heavy burden; an
   easier trip.
Jacking up one's spirits.
Jacked up.

JAIL
Feeling confined or feeling at the effect of your life rather
   than at its cause.

JAM
The sweetness of life.
Feeling you are in a "jam."
Traffic jams or log jams signify delays, confusion, and frustration; feeling stuck with no way to turn.
Take time to be still and reassess your life's situations.

JAR
See "Bottle."
A "jarring" experience.

JAW
Communication; to "jaw" or talk comfortably with friends.
If tightly closed, there is a need for more open communication.
Scolding; boring; long-winded.
A square jaw connotes strength, toughness.

JEALOUSY
Not feeling included; feeling left out.
Work on knowing that you are complete and whole exactly the way you are now; your presence is enough; there is nothing more that you need to be, do, or have in order to be whole.

JELLY
See "Jam."

JELLYFISH
Floating; drifting along.
No backbone.

JESUS
See "Christ."

JEWEL
Wealth; abundance; brilliance.
Inner treasures.

JOG
A reminder; "jogging" the memory.
Movement; self-betterment.
Jogging in place without getting anywhere.

JOURNEY
Self-exploration and growth.

JUDAS
A betrayal—usually, self-betrayal; not being true to yourself.

JUDGE
Self-judgment.
It may be directed at another but likely is something you
    have judged within yourself. (Remember, everything
    that you have done to others was necessary to get to
    where you are now. It was necessary for your growth.
    Holding this viewpoint helps you release judgment and
    guilt.)
May be a guide or your higher self giving you information.

JUGGLER
Trying to juggle many things at once.
If the juggler is doing a good job, so are you.
If the juggler is somewhat out of control, eliminate some
    things from your life; take time to assess what is really
    important in your life.

JUICE
"Juice up" or give life and energy.

Virile strength; vigor.
Provocative or racy.
Drunk.

JUMP
Leaping to a new venture; getting ahead.
Look before you leap.

JUNK
That which you no longer need, such as ideas, feelings, habits, relationships, etc.
To get rid of junk in your emotions, get rid of junk in your life. (The symbolic act of cleaning cupboards and drawers and getting rid of things that you don't use or don't love contributes to getting rid of emotional states that aren't contributing to who you really are.)

JURY
Self-criticism. Note the judgments that you feel the jury is making. Most often, these are judgments you have made about yourself. (Remember, what you have done and who you have been was necessary for you to be who you are today. Your life is unfolding perfectly for your evolution.)

KANGAROO
Restless energy.
Mobility.

KEY
A powerful symbol of opening doors for yourself on both the spiritual and the physical plane.

KEYHOLE
Being close to a solution or to a new direction in life, but not quite there. (Go back into your dream and imagine that

you are taking a key and opening the door. This will assist your waking life.)

KIDNAPPING
Self-sabotage.
Feeling out of control in a situation or at the effect of a situation; feeling the victim of a situation.
If a child is kidnapped, it may reflect a taking away of your inner child.

KIDNEYS
Fear.
Disappointment.
Criticism.

KILLING
Killing someone may be a sign that you are releasing parts of yourself that aren't necessary in your present evolution; killing off beliefs or behaviors that are no longer needed by you.
Killing a child most likely refers to killing off your own inappropriate childish behaviors, or it can be the death of your inner child.
Killing a parent may indicate getting rid of the way you have related to your parents or to your own parenting style.
Do not feel guilty if you have a killing dream; it usually signifies the beginning of a great spurt of self-growth.
A positive symbol.
If you are being killed, it is likely that you need to take control in your life so that you feel empowered rather than powerless. (Go back into your dream and do battle with your antagonist and win! This will help you in waking life.)

KING
Power and majesty; God.
Self-responsibility; taking charge of your own life.

KISS
Deep communion with self.
Warmth; affection; love.
Aligning the masculine and feminine aspects within ourselves.

KITE
Incredible spiritual soaring, yet grounded and anchored.
Childlike freedom.

KNEES
Fear.
Inflexibility; not wanting to give in.
Being in awe of, or worshiping, as in kneeling.

KNIFE
A powerful symbol either creatively or destructively.
The cutting away of that which isn't needed anymore, as in
    cutting the thorns from a rose; the cutting away of old pat-
    terns of thinking and being.
If someone is chasing you with a knife or knifing you, you
    may be in fear of being penetrated emotionally, physically,
    or sexually.

KNITTING
Tying ideas and life themes together; unifying.
Domestic peace.
Mending; repairing; the broken bone was "knitting."

KNOCK
An awareness trying to make itself known to you.
Opportunity knocking.

KNOT
Tension; tied up in "knots"; a stomach in "knots."
Making a commitment; tying the "knot."

Untying a knot signifies finding a solution or relaxation in a certain area of your life.

LABORATORY
Finding solutions through experimentation.

LABYRINTH
Winding through intricate passageways may signify feeling that there is no way out. The solution to being in a labyrinth is to stop and still your mind. Let your intuition come through, and the way out of your difficulty will become clear.

LAKE
A still, clear lake refers to intuition and deep inner wisdom.
Choppy water indicates emotional turmoil.
A cloudy lake signifies stagnant emotions.

LAMB
Sacrifice; martyrdom.
Easily led.
Purity, innocence.

LAMP/LANTERN
Inner light.
See "Light."

LAND
Solid grounding; your foundation.

LARGE INTESTINE
Release of toxic matter; release of that which you do not use or need.
Freedom of movement.
Assimilation.
Courage; having the guts to go forward.

LASER
Pinpointed consciousness; intense focus and concentration.

LAUGHTER
This is a great healer; don't take life so seriously.

LAUNCHING
Beginning a new venture.

LAUNDRY
Personal cleansing.
Cleaning up your "act."
Airing your dirty laundry.

LAVA
Something that has been suppressed for a long time, usually
   anger.

LAWN
Nurturing; grounding.

LEAPING
See "Jumping."

LEATHER
Strength; tough as "leather."

LEAVES
Green leaves: abundance; growth; life.
Yellowing leaves or leaves on the ground: completion; letting
   go; releasing.

LEGS
Feeling that you do not have a leg to stand on.

LEECH
Something is taking your strength or property or you are
   taking advantage of someone else.

LEMON
Cleansing and purifying.
Poorly constructed.

LEOPARD
Prowess; cunning; stealth.
Ferocity; valor; power.

LEPROSY
Wasting away; deteriorating.
Note which part of the body is affected.

LETTER
Information; news.
Indirect communication.

LIBRARY
Knowledge; inner knowing.
A powerful symbol.

LIFEGUARD
Often, a dream guardian or your higher self leading you
   through an emotional crisis.

LIGHT
The spiritual light within.
(The quality of the light signifies that of which we are aware
   in life.)

LIGHTNING
A potent symbol of great power; a breakthrough ahead.
Speed; strength.
Awakening of the kundalini life force.

LILY
Rebirth; life, death, and rebirth; transformation.

LION
King of the jungle; majesty; power; bravery; leadership.
Test of courage. (In some African tribes, part of the rite of
    manhood concerned pitting one's strength against a lion's.)

LIZARD
Earthy; primordial; steady.
Considered guardians of the inner worlds by the Aborigines.

LIVER
Anger.

LOCKING
Locking up something indicates a need for more self-
    acceptance.
Locking something up within yourself that you find undesirable.
Being in a house or other structure and locking others out
    means shutting yourself away from the realities of the
    world; locking out other people.

LUNGS
Grief.
Taking in life; the breath of life; taking charge of your life.
Needing breathing space.

MACHINERY
Feeling out of touch with the organic process of life.
Use of natural forces for power and strength.

MAGICIAN
Illusion; not real.

The tarot meaning is realizing aspirations by reaching inner resources; the magician is the transformer and the manifestor.

Magic comes from the ancient word *magh*, meaning "power"; the magician symbolizes channeling power from the inner realms to the outer realms.

MAGNET
Irresistible attraction.

MALE
The male part of the self; the yang energy; the masculine energy within; projecting energy.

MAN
The male part of yourself; the linear, rational, practical part of yourself; focused conscious awareness.

MANDALA
A circle or a mandala signifies harmony, beauty, balance.

A very powerful symbol; often used as a visual aid in meditation and religious worship.

MAP
Planning your journeys—inner and outer.

MARRIAGE
Uniting the male and female sides of yourself; integrating various aspects of self.

A uniting or coming together of ideas or people.

MARSH
Emotionally stagnating; unsure of yourself emotionally.

MARTYR
Lack of personal power; feeling that you are a victim of life's circumstances.
Giving to others and feeling resentful when you do not get sufficient appreciation.
A need to work on self-acceptance; accept responsibility for the circumstances in your life.

MASK
Different aspects of yourself.
Dishonesty.
Protection; concealment; non-being.

MASSAGE
Personal integration.

MATCH
Unlit: potential not yet revealed.
Lit: your inner light beginning to shine forth.

MAZE
See "Labyrinth."

MEADOW
A place of spiritual harmony and balance.
Rejuvenation; nurturance.

MEAT
The essence or "meat" of the matter.

MEDICINE
Healing.
Getting some of your own "medicine."

MELONS
Wholeness.
Something full of opportunity.

MENSTRUATION
Releasing the old; new beginnings.
If blood is evident, feeling loss of life energy.

MERCURY
Messenger of the gods; the bearer of messages.
God of trade, commerce, gain, luck, travel, and good gifts.
Eloquence.
Rapid changing of moods.

MERMAID
Your intuitive emotional self.
Unobtainable lover.
Temptation.
Connection with deep emotions and the subconscious.

MERRY-GO-ROUND
Feeling like you are going around and around without
    making any progress.

METAL
Strength; hardness.
Immobility.

MICROSCOPE
Intense self-examination.

MILK
Mother's milk; nurturance; sustenance.
"Milk" of human kindness.

MINE
Inner treasures undiscovered.

MIRROR
A step away from reality; a reflection of what is.
Truth; self-realization.

MISCARRIAGE
A miscarriage of justice.
Plans aborted or not fulfilled.
See "Abortion."

MISSING THE BOAT/PLANE/TRAIN
Feeling a lack of progress in your life; feeling left out because
   of the circumstances in your life.
Lost opportunity.
Not making enough of an effort; take time to reassess your
   goals.

MOLE
Burrowing.
Something beneath the surface; something not willing to be
   seen.

MONASTERY
Inward spiritual retreat.
May refer to a withdrawal from the world.

MONEY
Coins: a change coming in your life.
Wealth of experience, finances, etc.

MONSTER
An unacknowledged part of yourself that you fear; your
   hidden fears made manifest.

Examine your monster(s). The greatest fear is of the unknown. Become familiar with your dream monster. Ask yourself what parts of yourself it represents. You might even ask the monster what it represents.

Confront a threatening monster: instead of being victimized, imagine yourself going back into your dream and doing battle. Emerge victorious and ask the monster for a gift that is either valuable or beautiful.

MOON
The feminine aspect of yourself.
Inner emotional peace.
Full moon: wholeness and creativity from an intuitive base.
New moon or a crescent moon: a time of feeling at one with our internal spiritual self; a time for deep inner reflection.

MOTH
Perseverance beyond reason.
Something being eaten away without your awareness.

MOTHER
May reflect that part of yourself that your mother represents.
Nurturance; Mother Earth; that wiser, female part of yourself.
Divine Mother.

MOUNTAIN
An attainable goal or opportunity.
Going up the mountain: you are progressing toward your goal.
Going down the mountain: you are moving away from your goal.
A spiritually uplifting experience; monasteries and lamaseries are in the mountains because mountains are a place of spiritual retreat.
Don't make a mountain out of a molehill.
Can be viewed as an obstacle or an opportunity.

MOURNING
Letting go of habits, attitudes, and relationships that no longer
    serve you in order to make way for more appropriate ways
    of being.
Releasing.

MOUSE
Feeling of insignificance.
Temerity; fear.
A need for quiet; a concern about being quiet.

MOUTH
Communication; expressing yourself.

MOVIES
Observing life.
Becoming caught up in the drama of life.
The different roles in your life.

MUD
Feeling stuck; not moving or growing.
Things seem "muddy" in your life, not clean.
"Mud, mud, glorious mud" that a child enjoys; childlike joy.

MULE
Stubbornness.
Ability to carry heavy burdens.

MURDER
See "Killing."

MUSEUM
See "Home/House."
Knowledge; bringing wisdom from the past and assimilating it
    into the present.

MUSIC

Beautiful, harmonious music: uplifting spiritual alignment; inner harmony.

Music out of tune: feeling out of tune with your life.

MUSICAL INSTRUMENTS

Piano: the keys of life.

Flute: nature or freedom or the child within.

Drums: primitive nature or primordial instincts; staying with the beat; marching to a different drum.

Harp: celestial alignment; angels.

Harmonica: the wandering minstrel; time with friends; enjoyment; contentment.

Bagpipes: cultural fellowship.

Violin or strings: dedication; the sitar reflects Eastern culture; mysticism; internal peace.

NAIL

Carpenter's nail: support for larger structures; binding together.

Getting to the essence of the problem or "hitting the nail on the head."

Getting "nailed" or getting caught.

Chewing fingernails represents anxiety.

NAKEDNESS

Total freedom.

Vulnerability; feeling exposed.

Exposing a situation; baring your soul.

Sensuality.

NAUSEA

Something is making you sick to your stomach.

Getting rid of what isn't wanted.

NAVEL
The silver cord that connects your astral body to your physical
   body.
In the Orient, the center of the universe.

NECK
Positive: flexibility; being willing to see both sides of a
   situation.
Negative: a pain in the neck.
Being stiff-necked or immovable.

NEST
Incubating ideas or projects.
Nesting; home and family life; domestic life.
Pulling inward for rejuvenation.

NET
Feeling caught in a web or net of your own perception of
   reality. (Take time to still your mind and allow myriad
   other realities to be made available to you so that you
   can choose one that is more in alignment with who
   you truly are.)
Fishing net or butterfly net: help in catching things that are
   needed in life.
Safety net: catches you when you feel out of balance.

NIGHT
Obstacles; delays; not seeing things clearly; not being in touch
   with your inner knowing.
Clear night with visible stars or moonlight: a symbol of your
   intuition and your inner realms.

NIGHTMARE
Nightmares should be viewed as positive experiences. They
   allow us to deal with unresolved issues in daily life that

we are not allowing into our consciousness. These unresolved issues affect every aspect of life, including our
health and relationships. The nightmare is our subconscious way of healing these unresolved issues. Celebrate
your nightmares!

Imagine going back into your nightmare and play it through a
few times. Change the circumstances so that there is a positive outcome from your dream. This will assist in healing
the unresolved area of your life that was the source of the
nightmare.

NOSE
Nosy.
Self-recognition.

NUDITY
See "Nakedness."

NUMB
Most often there is some external, physical cause such as
sleeping in an awkward position. Or, it may be that you are
cut off from your feelings or are suppressing something that
you fear.

NUMBERS
See chapter 26.

NUN
Pulling your energies inward.
Celibacy; spiritual attunement.

NURSE
Healing; caring; nurturing.

NUTS
New life; potential yet to unfold.

Abundance; gathering nuts for the winter.

A hard nut to crack.

NYMPH

Minor divinity of nature in mythology; mystical maiden that
dwells in the mountains, waters, and trees.

Joyous sexuality.

Immature insects; incomplete development or incomplete
metamorphosis.

OAK

Powerful strength; solidarity; steady progress.

OAR

A boat without an oar may indicate that you feel adrift in an
emotional dilemma.

Oars can mean feeling in control amid emotional imbalance.

OASIS

Refuge; place of rejuvenation.

OBITUARY

Release of old ideas, thought forms, and beliefs.

OBSERVATORY

Getting the bigger picture; seeing the deeper meaning
in life.

OCEAN

Calm ocean: great inner power and emotional and spiritual
balance.

Rough or choppy ocean: the need for courage to allow you
to move to calmer waters amid emotional upheaval.

Sea of life: tremendous intuitive power.

OCTOPUS
Tenacious; grasping.
Shy and retiring.

OFFICE
Production.
Linear thought processes; organization.

OFFICER
Authority.
Protection or guidance.
Conscience; punishment; self-righteousness.
May indicate guilt; you want to be punished or kept out of trouble.
An affirmation for accepting authority over your life.

OIL
Lubrication; smoothing out difficulties; pouring oil on troubled waters.
Anointing with oil is a blessing.
A greasy or oily personality.

OLIVE
Peace; the olive branch of peace.

ONION
Layers of consciousness.
Potential sadness.

ORCHESTRA
Synthesis; harmony; synergy.

ORGASM
Depends on the feelings associated with orgasm and whether you reached the orgasm.

Powerful alignment with your inner male and female energies; connection to your kundalini energy.
For a male to reach orgasm in sleep may indicate a need to
strengthen the prostate gland.
See chapters 19 and 15.

ORGY
Your creative force may be dissipating; focus on your
life goals.

ORPHAN
See "Abandoned."

OSTRICH
Avoidance of looking at something in life.

OTTER
Capricious; playful.
Fun-loving.

OVEN
An idea or project is incubating.

OWL
A powerful symbol of transformation.
Ability to see clearly where things seem dark.
Wisdom.

OYSTER
Guarded energy.
Hidden beauty; beauty developing unseen.

PACING
If you are pacing back and forth, you are uncertain as to your
life's direction. Take time to be still. Thinking about the

situation isn't always the best solution. As you take time to quiet your mind, the correct solution will gently rise to the surface.

PACK
Carrying a pack: something or someone or an idea that you are carrying around with you is not necessary; let it go.
Packing: preparation for a change in your life.

PACKAGE
Sending: you are letting go of something.
Receiving: you are acknowledging an unrecognized part of yourself.

PAINT
Note the color, then see chapter 25.
Redoing; making new.

PALACE
See Home/House.
Your sense of your true magnificence.

PAN
Greek god of shepherds and hunters who originated panpipes; the joy in nature.
Panning with a movie camera: getting the bigger picture.
Panning for gold: looking for the true essence of something.
Pan or cooking pot: incubating an idea.

PANDA
Tranquillity.
Lovable; cuddly.

PARACHUTE
You are protected.

PARADE
Being willing to be recognized particularly for your community efforts.
Each of the participants in the parade is an aspect of yourself.

PARENTS
Although family members' roles are changing dramatically, our soul memory holds stereotypical images of parents.
Fathers: authority; linear, rational thought processes; projecting force; yang energy.
Mothers: the yin principle of nurturance; the inner realms of intuition and magic.
May pertain to your experience of your parents or your parenting skills.
May represent the mother/father energy that dwells within you.

PARROT
Insincerity.
Copying; imitating; speaking another's words without thinking.
Symbol of the exotic, the jungle.

PARTY
Celebration.

PASSENGER
If you are the passenger, you are "along for the ride"; you are not deciding the direction, someone else is.

PASSPORT
Your ticket for change and for creating what you want in your life.

PATH
Straight and narrow path going upward: you are making

progress; you are in alignment with your life's goals and
purpose; you are staying on the path.
Crooked path: you are wandering off course; you are not
quite sure in which direction to go.

PATTERN
A sewing or an embroidery pattern may symbolize your usual
reality system, the one in which you are comfortable.
Changing patterns may indicate breaking out of old
patterns.

PAVEMENT
New pavement is new direction.
To pave is to make your way easier or smoother.

PEACH
Uplifting; vitality.

PEACOCK
Pride; vanity.
Confidence taken to the extreme.

PEDESTAL
Putting someone or yourself in a position of elevation or
seeing that one as "above you." This detracts from your
inner power because when you experience yourself as a
part of all things, nothing becomes higher or lower.

PEGASUS
Freedom; inner magic.
Winged inspiration.
Soaring strength.

PEN
Expressing yourself fluidly; communication.
All "penned" up; feeling restricted.

PENCIL
Ability to express yourself; less restrictive than a pen.

PENDULUM
Uncertainty; weighing several choices.
Needing to find a balance in your life.

PENIS
Yang; projecting energy; the male principle; power; potency.

PEPPER
Spicy emotions.
Stimulating.

PERFUME
If you can actually smell perfume in your dream, it may represent sensuality.

PERISCOPE
Subconscious observation of conscious reality.
Objective observation.
If the periscope is in water, it means that you are observing your conscious reality from your emotional, intuitive self.

PETAL
Petals falling from the flower: sadness.
Pulling petals off a flower: "He loves me, he loves me not."

PHOTOGRAPHY
Objective observation of a situation.
Memories.

PIANO
See "Musical Instruments."
If a piano is out of tune, you are not in tune with yourself.

PIE
An opportunity; "getting a piece of the pie."
The round shape suggests wholeness combined with nourishment.
A whole with the possibility of being divided into shares.

PIG
Overindulgence.
Selfish; grasping.

PILL
Something unpleasant or repugnant that must be endured.
Someone disagreeable or tiresome; a real "pill."
Healing.

PILLAR
Strength.

PILLOW
Intuition; inner realms.
Relaxation; letting go.

PIN
Solid material that fastens separate articles together; a support that allows one article to be suspended from another.
A petty annoyance.
Getting "pinned down"; held fast or immobile.

PINE
Cleanser and purifier.
To "pine away" for someone or something.

PIONEER
Entering new areas within yourself and in your daily life.

PIPE
As a musical instrument: joy and freedom.
As a solid structure that conducts liquids or gases: the flow of energy within yourself and the universe.
The peace pipe of the Native American: an object of holiness and reverence, symbolizing unity with Spirit.

PIRATE
Unauthorized use of another's product, conception, or creativity.
You need to be your own authority in your life.

PIT
See "Abyss."

PLANETS
Heavenly bodies; illumination.
The rhythm of the universe.
Earth: grounding; nurturance.
Jupiter: expansiveness; vastness. A huge, imposing connotation.
Mars: aggressiveness; passion. A warlike connotation.
Mercury: the Greek messenger of the gods; communication and speed; swift change of mood.
Neptune: the god of the sea; psychic awareness; mysticism.
Pluto: small; concentrated; a spiritual unfolding; capricious joy as found in the Disney character of that name.
Saturn: sardonic; slow to act; a feeling of coldness.
Uranus: hidden abilities; changes.
Venus: beauty; harmony; femininity; gentleness.

PLASTIC
Flexibility; capacity to be molded or shaped; pliable.
Artificial; bogus.

PLATFORM
Taking a stand.
Stating your beliefs; a declaration of your principles.

PLAY
Children at play reflect joy and spontaneity.
"All the world's a stage. . . ."; your life is your script and *you* can choose to become involved in the drama or not; you can choose the script; it's all your play.

POCKET
A place of safekeeping.
A cavity containing something of value; a receptacle or container.

POISON
Something destructive or harmful—most often, an attitude about yourself; a fear or judgment.

POKER
You are gambling with something.

POLICE
See "Officer."

POND
Any area of water represents emotions and intuition. A calm, clear pond suggests calm, clear emotions. Troubled water suggests problems.
The boundaries of a pond are smaller than those of an ocean or a lake, indicating less of an emotional concern.

POOL
More suggestive of intuition and the deep inner realms of self than are other bodies of water.

POPCORN
Lots of creativity and new ideas moving into manifestation; the kernels (ideas) are expanding.
Stale popcorn indicates an unsatisfactory ending.

PORCUPINE
Something prickly; prickly situation.
Something you want to stay away from.

PORRIDGE
An added-on part of yourself; an extension of yourself.
That which is not a part of your basic nature yet you consider it in relation to yourself.

PORT
Safety.
Depending on the condition of the water nearby, concerns various emotions.
Good wine; enjoyment with friends.

PORTRAIT
How you see yourself or think others see you.
Not necessarily your true nature.

POSTMAN
Messages; news.
Information from an outside source; guidance.

POT
Something you are cooking; may relate to nurturing.
Something you are creating.
Marijuana; a different level of consciousness; dependence on outer stimulation rather than inner resources.

POTTERY
Molding your life, attitudes, and beliefs.

PRAISE
Congratulations! You have done well.
You have earned something.

PREGNANCY
You are about to give birth to an idea, a feeling, or an
  emotion.
A new creative project; going in a new direction.
A desire to be pregnant.
A powerful symbol.

PREMONITION
Note: Most dreams that appear to be premonitions usually
  point to aspects of growth of the inner self; very rarely are
  they true enactments of the future.
As upsetting as dreaming of the death of a child may be, it is
  likely to signify the "death" or putting away of childish things
  in your life. The dream is not necessarily a premonition.
It takes practice to recognize a premonition dream from a
  symbolic, self-growth dream, but there are some things
  found in premonition dreams you can look for:
Usually, the colors are quite a bit brighter in a premonition
  dream.
Very often, there is a rounded or round object. This shape
  symbolizes the energy of prophecy, of premonition.
In a premonition dream, the symbol will repeat itself three
  times.
If you are not sure, ask for clarification in another dream.
The more comfortable you become with having premonitions in your dreams, the easier it will be for you to have
  this type of dream in the future.

PRESIDENT
You are your own authority.
Control; leadership.
Priest; spiritual authority.
Guidance; showing the way.

PRINCE
The most divine masculine part of yourself.
The masculine force in the universe, yang.

PRINCESS
The most divine feminine part of yourself.
The feminine force in the universe, yin.

PRINT SHOP
Communication.
A solution to the current problem.
Repeating the situation many times.

PRISON
Self-imposed bars; self-imposed confinement. (You always have
　　the key to let yourself out; the only person who can imprison
　　you is you.)

PRISONER
Limiting your own potential; self-confinement.
Fear.

PROFANITY
Unexperienced emotions within normal daily life.

PROP
Something supporting you temporarily until you step into
　　your own wisdom, judgment, or strength.

PROPHET
Guidance; teaching; divine direction.
The mystic; the visionary; the master.
Listen to what the prophet says to you.
A powerful symbol of guidance.

PROSTITUTE
Prostituting yourself; using your energy inappropriately; mis-
    using your creativity.
Draining of latent sexual energy.
Revealing sensuality.

PRUNE
Shriveled; dried up.
Old; an older person.

PUDDLE
Nuisance; small emotional difficulty that is bothering you.

PUMP
Getting those life-affirming energies going; awakening of the
    kundalini energy.
Sexuality; power; strength; potency.
Free-flowing from a pump: easy, free-flowing emotion.
Pumping without result: emotional constriction or restriction;
    priming the pump indicates opportunity ahead.

PUPPET
Manipulation; feeling manipulated or that you are manipu-
    lating others.
Giving away your power; not remembering that you are in
    control.

PURSE
Tied to another's purse strings.

PUZZLE
Not seeing the whole picture.
Each part of your life is a different part of the puzzle; a completed puzzle indicates unification.
Feeling puzzled; unsure; lacking clarity.
Take time to concentrate or focus your energy. The answer will be forthcoming.

PYRAMID
A powerful symbol of inner unification and alignment.
A symbol of initiation; you have moved to a new level of awareness and understanding of yourself.
You are open to guidance from the higher energies around you and from your higher self.

PYTHON
A significant symbol.
Kundalini energy: the life force within you.

QUAIL
Fear; to recoil in dread.

QUAKER
These people are viewed as generally very balanced; they can represent balance and a peaceful life.
Family unity and harmony.

QUARANTINE
Feeling isolated or in a state of isolation.
Feeling separate from your true nature.

QUARREL
Different aspects of yourself are at war. Visualize the two quarreling parties in your dream discussing each other's position with an attitude of understanding or of peace. This

will allow you to put at rest the parts of yourself that are quarreling.

QUARTZ
Transmitter; energy conductor.
Spirituality.
Clarity.

QUEEN
The powerful female energy within you; it has more strength and more power than "princess."
The wisdom of womanliness rather than the purity of girlhood.
The goddess within.

QUEST
A spiritual journey.
Spiritual yearning.

QUICKSAND
Fear; feeling like you are being pulled under. (The way to deal with quicksand in your life is to be still. Expand your horizons and your perspective. There is a way out of the difficulty in which you are involved. Become one with the quicksand so that there is nothing that is not you and nothing to which you are not open.)

QUILT
Domestic happiness.
Protection.
Patchwork quilt: different parts of yourself coming together to make a whole.

RABBI
Guidance; showing the way.
Teacher.

RABBIT
May indicate prosperity.
Temerity, fear.
Fertility; children.
Gentleness, softness.
Going fast with no organization; hopping from one thing to
    another.
Look before you leap.

RACE
The only person with whom you are competing is yourself.
    Slow down; enjoy the run; smell the flowers.

RADAR
Being able to see beneath the surface.
Attunement; intuition.

RADIO
Communication; guidance from another source.

RAGE
Allow the anger that has been held in for so long to be
    expressed. Rage expressed in a dream will allow you to
    release the rage that is being suppressed in your daily life.

RAGS
Feeling of poverty of spirit.

RAILINGS
Feeling your boundaries; being aware of your boundaries.
Holding on to railings for support.

RAIN
Cleansing; purifying; emotionally refreshing.
May indicate that you are going through an emotional time
    and a cleansing process.

RAINBOW
A very powerful symbol of joy, celebration, and completion.
You have made it through the emotional difficulty.

RAM
Masculine strength.
Pioneering spirit. (The ram is the symbol of initiation or initi-
ating energy. It is a new beginning.)

RAPE
Accepting someone else's reality as your own.
Feeling penetrated.
Loss of power and self-esteem; feeling "ripped off."

RAT
Betrayer; wrongdoer.
Letting things gnaw at you.
Judging yourself through others' perceptions.
A mess; a "rat's nest."

RAVEN
The unknown; death.
Flying into unknown parts of yourself.
Fear of the unknown.
A messenger from the other side.

RAZOR
Cutting through.
Separation; release.
A safety razor can signify mental clarity.

RECIPE
Combining the ingredients of your life so that there is unity.

RECORD
Feeling like you are going around and around; stuck in a rut

or a groove; same old attitudes; same old feelings; it is time
to step off the treadmill.

RED CROSS
The sign of healing; self-healing.

REDWOOD TREE
Strength; wisdom; grounded yet with spiritual aspirations.

REFRIGERATOR
Feeling emotionally closed off; frozen emotions; lack of
warmth.

REPAIR
Something in your life needs mending or repairing. (In
your daytime hours, repair whatever you were trying to
repair in the dream. This symbolic act can help "repair"
your life.)

RESCUE
You need to be rescued; not feeling in control of your life;
feeling that others are in control. (This comes from the
viewpoint of a victim. Remember, there are no victims,
there are only volunteers.) Begin to move to a place of
responsibility for your life and your environment.
Rescuing others: you feel that someone needs help.

RESTAURANT
Sustenance; nourishment.
Fellowship.

REVOLUTION
Different aspects of yourself are at war; usually suggests a
coming time of change. (When awake, move to resolution
of the rebellion or the revolt.)

REVOLVING DOOR
Opportunities are being missed or passed.
Feeling like you are moving around and around with old attitudes and ideas.

RHINOCEROS
A sexual symbol.
Powerful; forceful; charging ahead without stopping.

RICE
Domestic happiness; wedding; joy; celebration.
Good harvest.

RIDING
Riding an animal: a feeling of alignment with nature; mastery; conquest.
Riding in a vehicle while someone else is driving: you feel that you are not in charge of your life; someone else is guiding you.
You are being taken for a ride; being deceived.

RING
Long friendship; marriage; engagement.
Promise.
Eternal love.
Completion; wholeness; unity.

RIVER
The river of life; the flowing waters of life.
"Don't push the river, it flows by itself."
Trying to swim upstream; allow the river to carry you; don't fight the current.

You are trying to get across the river and you can't find the way. The river usually represents an emotional barrier you are having trouble crossing. (When awake, imagine a bridge across the river and walk to the other side. Make yourself a new route in order to resolve the situation.)

ROAD
Your direction in life.
Look carefully at the road. Is it rocky? Crooked? Straight? Does it go uphill or downhill? Is the way clear? (This represents your destiny, your direction in life. Look for forks in the road, forks representing major decisions to be made.)
The condition of the road suggests the way that you are running your life at this moment.

ROBBER
Tremendous fear and insecurity.
Feeling a victim of life. (Remember that the other side of *what is so* is, *so what!* There are no victims.)
Begin to take responsibility for your life; accept responsibility for it.
Go back into your dream and defeat the robber. Become the hero or heroine of your dream and you will move toward greater strength and security within yourself.

ROBIN
A very fortunate omen.
Harbinger of good things.
New beginnings.

ROBOT
Mechanical feelings.
Feeling of being shut off from your feelings; unfeeling.

ROCK
Grounding; strength; personal power.
The rock of Gibraltar.

ROCKET
Soaring to spiritual heights; unlimited potential and power.

ROOF
Your protection; this corresponds to your crown chakra.
The condition of your roof suggests the condition of your
    spiritual connection.
See "Home/House."

ROOM
An aspect of yourself.
See "Home/House."

ROPE
An attachment to a person, place, or thing.
Your kundalini power.
A lifeline.
Neatly coiled rope: organization; inner twining and balancing
    of mind, body, and soul.
Frayed or knotted rope: dissociation.
Feeling tied up; feeling in knots; feeling restricted.

ROSE
Love; beauty; innocence.

ROW
A fight; an argument.
May represent organization; soldiers in a row.

ROWING
Moving through an emotional situation.

ROYALTY

Depending on whether it is male or female, this relates to the divine aspects of self; the divine feminine; the divine masculine.

Feeling a sense of your own royalty, your own divinity.

RUNNING

Stop! Turn around; face the truth.

Running from a situation you are not ready for; feeling unsure of yourself; fear of a situation or experience you are not willing to acknowledge. (Turn around and face the antagonist, whether in your dream or when awake, and as you face that from which you are running, you will begin to dissolve that barrier in your daily life.)

Running in slow motion: the time is coming soon when you will have to face that difficulty.

Running toward something: you are in a time of great acceleration within your spiritual life; celebrate.

RUST

Talents or abilities not being used.

You are a bit rusty in your skills; polish up those talents and abilities.

SACK

Future events yet to be revealed.

Hiding or self-concealment.

Getting "sacked"; losing your power.

SACRIFICE

Someone or something being sacrificed: an area of your life where you feel that you are making a sacrifice. (This is martyrdom. See "Martyr.")

Feeling at the mercy of life rather than in control of it. (You are in control of your destiny. Affirm, "I choose my life

and I choose it completely. I am in control of my life. I
have chosen my life's circumstances."

SADDLE
Feeling bound; feeling saddled to a situation that you wish to
be free of.

SAILBOAT
Navigating through emotional change.
Moving quickly and easily: soaring through emotional change
with ease.

SAINT
Your guardian angel or protector; your higher self.
Listen very carefully to the messages and notice the symbols
that occur in this dream.

SALMON
The sacred fish of the Celts.
Moving ahead against all odds.

SALT
The salt of the earth.
The element earth.
Strength and stability.

SAND
The sands of time; nothing is permanent; everything is an
illusion.
A house built on sand, not on a permanent foundation.
Changes; things changing.
Irritations; small, temporary annoyances.

SAW
Cutting one down to size; construction; building; creating;
making; doing.

Pruning.

An emotional wound from the past that is healing but is still not forgotten. (Check the other symbols, people, and situations to identify the emotional scarring that still needs to be healed.)

SCARECROW

Not real; false; being afraid; scared.

As in the *Wizard of Oz*, not much intellectual ability.

Scaring people off with a false front or false appearance.

SCHOOL

The school of life; those lessons you have chosen for yourself in this lifetime.

Allow the environment and life to be your teacher; let each circumstance and each person be your teacher; let them show you the way.

SCIENTIST

Left-brained; analytical; thinking; rational; intelligent; let the heart rule as well as the head.

SCISSORS

Cutting away; releasing that which is unnecessary in your life.

Feeling cut off from others or from yourself.

SEA

See "Ocean."

SEAM

Coming apart at the seams.

That which binds things together.

SEASONS

See chapter 22.

SEEDS
Great things grow from small beginnings, provided they have
    all the right ingredients.
A new beginning.
"As you sow, so shall you reap."

SEESAW
Feeling that you are going up and down but not getting
    anywhere.

SEMEN
Power; potency; strength; the creative potential.

SEX
See chapter 15.

SHADOW
The latent potential of an individual.
Fear; illusion.
The unknown part of yourself.

SHAPES
If there are undefined shapes in a dream, when you're awake
    say, "What does that shape remind me of? What feeling do
    I have about this shape?"
Allow the shape to take form. It can be something unformed
    or not quite solidified within your life. If you allow the
    shape to take form in your imagination, soon that project,
    idea, or feeling will begin to take shape in your life.

SHARK
Omen of danger.
Hidden fear.
Cruel misuse of power.

SHAVE
A close shave; a close call.
Grooming; bolstering self-confidence.

SHEEP
Following without using your judgment.
Nonthinking trust.
Being taken advantage of monetarily; being "fleeced."

SHELL
Emptiness; an empty shell.
Pulling into your shell; closing off from the outer world; non-
    activity; nongrowth.

SHEPHERD
Guardian of the spirit; guardian of the inner way.

SHIELD
Your protection, allowing you to stay balanced and centered
    amid change.
May symbolize a defense mechanism.

SHIP
Yourself, your whole self, when life is uncertain, particularly
    in regard to emotions.
See "Boat."

SHOES
Steps to be taken in life.
Grounding; connecting to the earth.
Don't judge another until you walk in his shoes.
Filling too many shoes; filling too many roles.

SHOULDERS
Shouldering your responsibilities; shoulder to the wheel.

SHOOTING
Shooting at a target: focusing energy for a particular goal.
Shooting someone: killing off an aspect of self.
Being shot: feeling penetrated; the victim.

SHOPPING
Decisions; choices.

SHOULDER
Strength.
Accepting responsibility;
Putting your "shoulder to the wheel."

SHOWER
Emotional cleansing; cleaning up your act.

SILK
Luxuries; riches; wealth.
Sensuality; ability to flow.

SILVER
Second best.
May be the silver cord; spiritual connection.
Inner light.

SINGING
Celebration; joy; uplifting of spirit; spiritual light.
Troubles are over; harmony.

SISTER
Female aspect of self.
Religious aspect; nun.
Relatedness; sisterhood.

SKELETON
Things unacknowledged; a skeleton in the cupboard.

Doesn't necessarily mean physical death; can mean emptiness; devoid of content.

SKIING
Exhilaration.
If you are going too fast, may be a sign that you are going too fast in life; feeling out of control.
Using your skills to master the difficulties in your life.

SKUNK
Social disapproval.
Something "smells."

SKY
The heavens; no limitation to success; the sky is the limit.
Freedom; expansion.

SLAVE
Being a slave to old habits, ideas, or beliefs.
A slave to other people, other situations.

SLEEPING
Dreaming that you are sleeping may mean that you are astral traveling and observing yourself from outside your body.
Unwillingness to change; stagnation.
Not moving; not changing.

SLIDE
Feeling out of control.

SMOKE
Where there is smoke, there is fire; a warning of danger.
Lack of clarity; things are confused.

SNAIL
Things are moving slowly; going at a "snail's pace."
Break out of your shell; get going!

SNAKE
A very significant symbol that is not to be feared.
Healing; life potency; the power within; kundalini power.
Spiritual awakening; spiritual healing.
Feeling tempted or wanting to tempt someone.
"Snake in the grass."

SNOW
Cleansing.
Purity; a fresh start; a new look at the world; a new beginning.
Frozen, blocked emotions.

SOAP
Cleansing; purification.

SOLDIERS
War within and without.
Organization; discipline.

SPEEDOMETER
Going too fast; going too slow.
Look at the numbers on the meter, then see chapter 26.

SPERM
See "Semen."

SPHINX
Spiritual understanding.
May signify past-life recognition from Egypt.

SPIDER
Industry.
The eight legs of the spider signify material wealth; wealth through industry.
Trap; entrapment; getting caught in your own web.

SPIRAL
The image of evolution.
That intricate component of all of life, the DNA and RNA helix.
A very powerful transformational symbol.

SPIRIT
A ghost from the past; a haunting memory.

SPONGE
Soaking up everything; learning indiscriminately.
Sponging off other people; feeling others are sponging off you.

SPRING
See chapter 22.

SPY
Feeling unsafe.
Being intruded on or intruding on others.
Involvement with another person rather than with your development.

SQUARE
Stability.
Old-fashioned; not in touch with the times; out of step.
Boxed in; controlled.

SQUIRREL
Frugality; comfort through patience.

STAG
Sexual vigor.
Powerful; potent.

STAGE
The stage of life.
The role you play in life.
How you feel you appear to others or are seen by others.

STAIRS
Ascending: a rise in status; success. Descending: loss of recog-
     nition; loss of confidence.

STAR
A significant symbol of light, guidance, and insight.
You are your own star; you are your own light.

STATUE
Frozen feelings and emotions.
Feeling immobile; you can't move.
Lifeless.
Not coming from your own strength and your own energy.
Needing to work on self-confidence.

STEEL
Strength; immobility; inflexibility.
Determination.

STOMACH
Just can't stomach it.
Stomach holds nourishment; helps you digest attitudes, ideas,
     feelings.
May indicate an inability to assimilate that which is new; fear
     of the new.

STONES
Leave no stone unturned.
See "Rock."

STORK
New beginnings; new arrival.
Conception; birth of a new idea.
May be an omen of domestic happiness and contentment.

STRAW
"This is the last straw."
Insubstantial: as in a "house of straw."
"The straw that broke the camel's back."

SUCKING
Nursing; nurturing.
If you are nursing a baby, you are nurturing new ideas, a new
    way of being.
If you are being suckled, you are being given sustenance and
    nurturing.

SUICIDE
Self-guilt; self-persecution.
Killing off aspects of yourself.
Giving up.
A warning not to give up; know that you are never given
    anything in life that you can't handle, do, or accomplish.
A sign to reach out for help from those around you; pray.

SUMMER
See chapter 22.

SUN
God; Great Spirit; Christ; the god within.
The source from which all flows.
Power; strength; clarity.
Your inner light.

SUNFLOWER
Joy.
Embracing life.

SWAMP
Feeling completely bogged down, with absolutely no clarity;
   no way to get out; feeling overwhelmed or swamped with
   work.

SWAN
The sign of the white goddess.
Beauty.
Strength.
Gliding to new heights; freedom.
A black swan may be a sign of the inner mysteries of life;
   intuition.

SWEETS
The sweetness of life.
Lovers.
Honoring oneself.

SWIMMING
Don't swim against the current.
Stay afloat amid emotional changes.

SWORD
Defense.
Attack.
Power; truth; honor.
Slaying the ego, inner demons, or illusions.

SYRUP
Overly sentimental; overly emotional to the point of insincerity.
Stickiness.

TABLE
Putting off a decision; tabling a decision or an emotion; beliefs
    that are clearly seen by others.
Putting your cards on the table.

TAPE
Playing the same problems over and over again; stuck in the
    same pattern.
Taping things together may represent unity or unification.

TAPESTRY
The tapestry of life; each part of the tapestry represents a dif-
    ferent part of you.

TARGET
Your direction; your goal.
Self-focus and self-discipline are needed.

TAX
Burden.
Being taxed to your limit; the taxing of your strength.

TEA
Friendship.
Relaxation.

TEACHER
The guru within.

Self-reliance.

Each person in our life is our teacher; each aspect within a dream is our teacher during the night.

TEARS
Release; cleansing; balancing.

TEETH
Chewing; preparing for digestion.

Biting into a problem.

Chewing the fat; talking; discussing.

If teeth are falling out, it may mean talking too much; scattering your energy; not understanding a problem or situation.

Loss of teeth may reflect a loss of face; a spoiling of the appearance in some way; a loss of power; keeping your mouth shut because you are talking too much. (According to Edgar Cayce, meant careless speech, and false teeth signified falsehood.)

An infected tooth signifies foul language.

Teeth stand for decisiveness; loss of teeth symbolizes loss of the power of decisive action.

Loss of teeth may symbolize growing up; moving to a new stage of development; a new stage of life as baby teeth are replaced by permanent teeth.

Loss of teeth may indicate dental problems; check with your dentist.

TELEGRAM
Staying in touch with the world around you.

A message from afar or from estranged part of yourself.

TELEPHONE
Listen to others.

May indicate a guide who is trying to get your attention;
   listen carefully to the message.
Telephone dreams are important.

TELESCOPE
Farseeing, but not all is revealed.

TEMPLE
Private retreat; inner sanctuary.

TENT
Impermanence; temporary.
The image of self is not solidified.

THREAD
Karma; fate.
A thread of truth.

THROAT
Positive; being willing to speak your own truth.
Negative: feeling strangled.
Can't swallow it.

THUNDER
Release of suppressed emotions and feelings.
The warning voice of the gods.
Anger; hostility; rage; the aftermath of a powerful emotional,
   psychic release.

TIDAL WAVE
A huge emotional upheaval.

TIDE
The ebbing and flowing of your emotions.
The ebb and flow of life.

TIGER
Cunning; prowess.
Power; energy.

TIGHTROPE
Feeling tense.
Feeling as if you have to walk a tightrope; great pressure;
   stress.

TIRES
Mobility; movement.
A flat tire means you are not balanced.

TOILET
Elimination of that which isn't needed in your life.

TOMB
Transformation, death, and resurrection.
Restriction.

TOWER
Isolation; being locked in an ivory tower; cut off from dif-
   ferent aspects of yourself.
May represent spiritual point of clarity.
Spiritual vision.

TOY
Joy; life is play.
Feeling that you are being toyed with.

TRAIN
The collective and individual journey through stages and
    events of your life.
Power.
The "Little Engine That Could."

TRASH
Junk; emotional junk that you are carrying around; letting go
    of it; eliminating it; releasing it.

TREADMILL
Feeling that you are getting nowhere; you are stuck with the
    same beliefs, attitudes, and thoughts.

TREASURE
Original ideas; personal wealth.
Inner wealth; gifts from Spirit.

TREES
Family matters; a family tree.
Life's development.
Feeling rooted and grounded on the earth plane yet soaring to
    spiritual heights.
Old gnarled tree: wisdom; strength.
Slender willow tree: being able to bond with circumstances.
Aspen: fear; quaking with fear.
Oak: strength.
Pine: spiritual clarity; purification.
Cedar: clarity; spirituality.
Apple: see "Apple."
Other fruit tree: bearing fruit in life.
Palm: warmth; freedom.
The meaning can depend on whether the tree is just begin-
    ning to leaf, is in full leaf, is losing its leaves, or has no
    leaves. (See chapter 22.)
Is the tree straight or crooked? As the tree bends, so it grows.

TRIANGLE
Trinity; protection; body, mind, and spirit.
Integration.
Power of the pyramids.

TUNNEL
Light at the end of the tunnel.
Inner passageway to the self.
Tunnel vision; close-mindedness.
An out-of-body experience (Very often you will have a dream of moving through a tunnel.)
May signify a near-death experience; changing realities; changing levels of consciousness.

TURTLE
A powerful symbol.
Slow but steady progress toward the goal.
Completion through diligence.
May signify a wish or a need to withdraw from a problem and go inward to gather forces.

UFO
Personal integration; psychic potential; higher intelligence.
Fear of the unknown; fear of unknown aspects of yourself.

UMBRELLA
Protection; being sheltered from life's storms.

UNCLE
Cry "uncle"; give up.
Feeling foolish; being a "monkey's uncle."
May refer to your uncles.

UNDERGROUND
Your unconscious; your subconscious.

UNDERTAKER
Undertaking an unpleasant situation or experience.

UNDRESSED
Feeling exposed.
Personal secrets being revealed; being open.

UNICORN
A powerful symbol.
Traditionally, the symbol of Christ; spiritual unfoldment; purity; virginity.

UNIFORM
Rigidity; inflexibility.
Authority.

UNIVERSITY
Center of learning.

UPPER LIP
Carrying on in spite of difficulties; keeping a stiff upper lip.

URINE
Relief from tension.
Emotional release; cleansing.
A need to relieve yourself.

URN
Ashes to ashes, dust to dust.
Reincarnation.

VACATION
Enjoyment; relaxation.
Letting go; release.
Take a new look at your ideas and goals.

VACCINATION
Emotional protection.

VACUUM
Feeling that you are living in a vacuum; feeling isolated; not feeling creative.
Clean or remove that which isn't needed; eliminate the negativity in your life.

VAGINA
Openness; acceptance; receptivity.
Womanliness.
The inner valley of the spirit.

VALLEY
The low point in life; the mountains and valleys in life.
A need to pull inward, feel sheltered for a time.

VAMPIRE
Exhaustion; draining of vitality by others.
Feeling exhausted.

VELVET
Sensuality; look to see what is beneath the surface.

VENTRILOQUIST
What you hear might be wrong or inaccurate information.
Voicing someone else's opinions rather than your own.

VETERINARIAN
Healing our animal nature.

VINE
A spiritual connection.

VINEYARD
Harvesting the fruits of our labors and experiences.

VIRGIN
Purity; chastity.
Mother Mary; the female aspect of God.
Newness; a fresh phase in life.

VOLCANO
Explosion of suppressed emotions.

VOMIT
Getting rid of that which you don't need; getting rid of old
   ideas, attitudes, and beliefs.
A need to express and communicate that which you are
   holding back or is making you sick.
Getting things out in the open.

VULTURE
Feeling there is something or someone waiting for you to
   make an error.
A need to clean away something that you consider complete
   or "dead."

WAITER/WAITRESS
Being of service to others or to yourself.

WALKING
Your goals will be met through a slow but sure pace.

WALL
An obstacle; a blockage.
Feeling walled off from others.

WALLET
The personal beliefs and thoughts that you hold privately.

WAND
Spirituality.
You can change things instantly; transformation.

WAR
Conflict; inner aggression.
Unresolved issues.

WAREHOUSE
Your potential; all that you ever need is within.

WASHING
Releasing the past; forgiving.
Letting go of old attitudes and beliefs.

WASP
Feeling threatened.
Stinging thoughts or words.

WATCH
The passage of time; time is passing.

WATER
Emotional energy; intuition.
Check to see whether the water is clear or murky.
Spiritual alignment and attunement; your unconscious self;
    the waters of life.

WATERFALL
Complete healing; emotional release.
Complete emotional recharging.

WAVE

Waving at someone or someone waving at you; love; connection; acknowledgment.

An ocean wave suggests surging forward; great strength and power.

Using your emotions creatively.

Watching waves symbolizes recharging your inner batteries.

WAX

Easily molded; the situation can be changed.

Cleaning; making a surface shiny; making something look new.

WEASEL

Treachery; betrayal.

Feeling someone is pushing you out of the way or "weaseling in" on your territory.

WEATHER

Your emotional state; your health.

Clear weather: excellent health.

Stormy weather: some area in your body may need alignment.

WEAVING

The pattern of your life woven in and out; the tapestry of your life.

Putting things together; creating wholeness.

WEB

Feeling caught; feeling entangled.

Beware a trap.

The pattern of your life: you are the weaver.

WEDDING

Union of your conscious and unconscious, of your body and spirit.

WELL
Inner riches; wisdom accumulated from past experiences.

WHALE
A significant symbol.
Perception; intuition.
Tremendous power and strength.
May concern the size of something; a "whale" of a job.
May indicate a cry for help, as in "wail."

WHEEL
The wheel of life.
The wheel of fortune.
The wheel of karma; sowing and reaping; endings and beginnings; completion; never-ending change.

WHISPER
Feeling held back.
Being unwilling or unable to communicate what is in your heart and mind.

WHISTLE
A warning; something is trying to get your attention.

WILLOW
Sadness.
Being able to bend and move as the situation warrants.

WIND
The winds of change.
The element of air, representing thought and intellect.
Messages from the realm of spirit.
Changing winds may signify changes coming up for you.

WINDOW
Interdimensional viewing; being able to see different levels of
   consciousness.
Seeing the future or the past.

WINE
Prosperity; abundance.
Celebration.
Relaxation.
Spiritual attunement, with wine representing the blood of
   Christ or the spiritual energy within; God.

WINGS
Freedom; soaring.

WITCH
The current implication of being fearsome or ugly.
The word *witch* came from "wicca," meaning "wise woman";
   may represent that wise female energy within you.

WOLF
Community and social feeling; family support.
Fear, especially concerning being pressed for something
   without the resources to meet the need; "wolf" at the door.
Inappropriate flirtatious behavior.

WOMB
Nourishment; safety; protection.
Pulling in your energies and regrouping before the next
   endeavor.

WORM
Hidden preparation or work beneath the surface.
Lowlife; no backbone.
Being intruded on; someone "worming" his way in.

X-RAY
Unseen forces.
Seeing what is within with more clarity, more understanding.
Inner depths; inner understanding.

YAWN
Boredom; need for another outlet for creativity.

YO-YO
Feeling that you are going up and down; repeating the same
patterns.

29.

STARTING A DREAM GROUP

A powerful way to connect more deeply with your dreams is to join a dream support group or start one yourself. A dream group consists of individuals who periodically meet to share and discuss their dreams. This provides encouragement and support in your dream journey.

Purpose

To form a dream group, first determine the purpose for the gathering. Perhaps you want to develop individual psychic abilities, or to process daytime difficulties through examining your theater of the night. Write down your intentions in clear, concise language so that each group member can consciously choose to be in alignment with the group's purpose. This first step is imperative and will enhance the synergy in future meetings. Decide on a time—perhaps once a week—when it is convenient for all members to attend.

Each dream group will have its own dynamics. However, here is a simple format that you might consider: For the first meeting, sit in a circle, then go around the circle, with each person sharing briefly about her- or himself. Each person should include personal information such as goals, purpose in life, and so on. Let the first meeting be a time for clarification of purpose and intent, as well as for developing the beginnings of synergy among all members of the group.

Grounding

Each time you gather, begin the session by devoting a few moments to centering and relaxing. (You may wish to have a leader for this process.) All members should sit in a circle, with their spines straight, feeling very relaxed. Form a grounding cord by imagining a silver light moving up from the earth, through the soles of your feet and the base of your spine and on up and out the top of your head, then cascading around you like a waterfall. After all members have completed this, begin breathing in the essence of each individual in the circle. Take a deep breath, breathing each person into your being, then slowly releasing that person. As you do this, imagine each person as strong, healthy, and well balanced. In doing so, you are weaving a deep spiritual connection among all the dreamers in the group. Next, breathe in the essence of your own being three times. Imagine a brilliant silver-white light spinning around the group, creating a whirlpool of energy and light. When everyone has completed this meditation, take just a few moments of silence before proceeding with the dream sharing.

Dream Sharing

In sharing around the circle, it is necessary that each person be given adequate time to share his or her dreams. If an individual feels that the events of the week are connected to the dream in some way, sharing these events may be valuable. It is important to keep in mind, however, that it is very easy to wander from the point, so others may be denied a chance to share. Also, before selecting a specific dream to work with, make sure everyone has had a chance to share. Not being able to share a dream simply because you have run out of time can be very disappointing. Since every dream is a composite of multitudes of complex images spanning several dimensions, it would be easy to invest several sessions on only one dream. Keep in mind the value of doing some work with each dream shared by those in the group.

When each member has the opportunity to communicate dreams, this begins to build a deep connection with the others in the group. As a result, you will experience a heightened sense of telepathy among the members and even a similarity of dream symbols.

When sharing your dream, always use the present tense rather than the past—"I am running" rather than "I was running." This enables you to be far more present with the dream as you communicate it to others. Also, speaking in the first person will usually make it easier to discover new insights about yourself. When an individual begins to share a dream using the present tense and then slips back into past tense, it generally indicates a point in the dream where there are difficult emotions. It is valuable to point this out to the dreamer. Occasionally this will enable the person to experience a revelation, an "Aha!"

Listen very carefully to the specific words a person uses in describing his or her experience. Also, closely observe the dreamer's body language as he expresses the dream.

Maintain the attitude that each dreamer in the group is a different reflection of yourself. As a dream's secrets unfold to the others, it will generate a new awakening within you. Listen carefully to the manner in which each person discusses the dream. Every dream will have a special significance for you. Each person's dream is also about you. You have all been drawn together because of similar energies. All the others in the dream group are present with you. For each session, have a leader who can keep the group on track. One means of doing this is to have a revolving leadership, with a different member in charge at each new meeting.

Dream Meanings

When a dream is selected to be explored more closely by the entire group, it is valuable for the person sharing the dream to hear insights from the group. However, it is crucial that the dreamer accept only what "feels right" regarding the others' interpretations.

If your group is an especially expressive one, you might have occasional "theme weeks." One week you may all decide to incubate for prophetic dreams concerning the coming year. Another week you might focus on emotional cleansing of blockages formed during childhood. If you are feeling especially whimsical, you might devote a week to telepathic communication with aliens. More practically, perhaps the theme of the week may be to analyze the actions of the stock market. You might also devote a week to healing— night healing, day healing, or self-healing.

Be creative in your dream groups. In one session you could all dance your dreams, while in another, come equipped with crayons and paper to draw your dreams. You might choose to select dream partners and dream for each other during the week, setting aside one specific evening for this purpose. I've discovered this last exercise to be especially powerful for me in gaining insights into myself. Often what is a blind spot for one dreamer is easily perceived by another. Even those with relatively little experience in dream work have been able to dream for another, unwrapping symbols extremely significant for that person.

Bring your dream journals to each session, sharing them freely with one another. You can also set apart a section in your journal where you note some of the insights given by others in the group. Other creative ways to explore your dreams are to construct a dream mask or dream shield. Also, the group as a whole could take a particularly significant dream and act it out as a play, with each member taking a different role in the dream script.

Set a specific starting time and closing time so that each member has some idea of how long he may take in sharing his dream. This plan ensures a sense of completion for each one in the group. And have fun!

THE ENDING

Row row row your boat
Gently down the stream
Merrily, merrily, merrily, merrily
Life is but a dream.

NOTES

CHAPTER 1   WHAT SCIENTISTS SAY ABOUT DREAMS

1. Sharon Begley, "The Stuff That Dreams Are Made Of," *Newsweek*, 14 August 1989, 41–44.
2. Michael E. Long, "What Is This Thing Called Sleep?" *National Geographic*, December 1987, 790–91.
3. Ibid., 787–88; 802.
4. Ibid., 791; 802; 818.
5. Jill Morris, *The Dream Workbook* (New York: Fawcett Crest, 1985), 15.
6. Ibid., 16.
7. Ibid.
8. Ibid., 13.
9. Ibid., 16–17.
10. Nerys Dee, *Your Dreams and What They Mean* (New York: Bell Publishing Company, 1984), 43–44. (UK edition: Aquarian Press, 1984.)
11. Long, 820.
12. Jeremy Taylor, *Dream Work* (New York: Paulist Press, 1983), 6. (UK distributor: Fowler Wright.)
13. Ibid., 6–7.
14. Ibid., 7.
15. Ibid., 7–8.

CHAPTER 2   WHAT PYCHOLOGISTS SAY ABOUT DREAMS

1. Nerys Dee, *Your Dreams and What They Mean* (New York: Bell Publishing Company, 1984), 56–57. (UK edition: Aquarian Press, 1984.)
2. Ibid., 57.
3. Ibid., 58–59.
4. Jean Dalby Clift and Wallace B. Clift, *Symbols of Transformation in Dreams* (New York: The Crossroad Publishing Company, 1987), 6–7.
5. Ibid., 7.
6. Ibid., 11–12.
7. Ibid., 12–13.
8. Dee, 62.
9. Clift and Clift, 9–10, and Dee, 62–63.
10. Clift and Clift, 14.
11. Ibid., 17.

CHAPTER 3   WHAT METAPHYSICIANS SAY ABOUT DREAMS

1. Harmon H. Bro and Hugh Lynn Cayce, ed., *Edgar Cayce on Dreams* (New York: Warner Books, 1968), 7.
2. Ibid.
3. Ibid., p. 8.
4. Ibid., 8–9.
5. Ibid., 16–19.
6. Ibid., 11–32.
7. Ibid.

CHAPTER 4   ANCIENT DREAMERS

1. Patricia Garfield, *Creative Dreaming* (New York: Ballantine Books, 1974), 215.
2. Ibid., 20–21.
3. Nerys Dee, *Your Dreams and What They Mean* (New York: Bell Publishing Company, 1984), 14. (UK edition: Aquarian Press, 1984.)
4. Ibid., 15.
5. Dee, 15–16; Jean Dalby Clift and Wallace B. Clift, *Symbols of Transformation in Dreams* (New York: The Crossroad Publishing Company, 1984), 90, and Ann Faraday, *The Dream Game* (New York: Harper and Row, 1974), 63.
6. Dee, 16, and Garfield, 24.

7. Garfield, 24–25.
8. Dee, 16–17.
9. Ibid., 17–18.
10. Ibid., 18.
11. As quoted in Garfield, 26.
12. Garfield, 26.
13. Dee, 18; 22.
14. Ibid., 23.
15. Ibid., 25–26.

CHAPTER 5 NATIVE DREAMERS

1. Patricia Garfield, *Creative Dreaming* (New York: Ballantine Books, 1974), 59–60.
2. Jeremy Taylor, *Dream Work* (New York: Paulist Press, 1983), 108. (UK distributor: Fowler Wright.)
3. Ibid.
4. Ibid., 108–9.
5. Ibid., 109.
6. Garfield, 69.
7. Ibid., 73.
8. Ibid., 71–72.

CHAPTER 7 DREAM AIDS

1. George Frederick Kunz, *The Curious Lore of Precious Stones* (Philadelphia: J. B. Lippincott Company, 1913), 176–224. (UK edition: Dover Publications, 1972.)

CHAPTER 8 DREAM INCUBATION

1. Patricia Garfield, *Creative Dreaming* (New York: Ballantine Books, 1974), 20–21.
2. Ibid., 21–23.

CHAPTER 9 LUCID DREAMING

1. Patricia Garfield, *Creative Dreaming* (New York: Ballantine Books, 1974), 151–69, and Stephen LaBerge, *Lucid Dreaming* (New York: Ballantine Books, 1985), 23–25; 144–45.
2. Michael E. Long, "What Is This Thing Called Sleep?" *National Geographic*, December 1987, 787.

CHAPTER 10   DREAM GAZING
1. Virgina Bass, ed., *Dreams Can Point the Way: An Anthology* (Sugar Land, Texas: Miracle House Books, 1984), 145.

CHAPTER 11   DREAMS FOR "SEEING"
1. Eve Loman, *You Are What You Dream* (Greenwich, Connecticut: Fawcett Publications, 1972), 61–62.

CHAPTER 12   DREAMS FOR PAST LIFE RECALL
1. Marcia Moore and Mark Douglas, *Reincarnation, Key to Immortality* (York Harbour, Maine: Arcane Publications, 1968), 17–31.

CHAPTER 13   DREAMS FOR ASTRAL TRAVEL
1. Carlos Castaneda, *Journey to Ixtlan* (New York: Simon and Schuster, 1972). (UK edition: Penguin, 1990.)
2. Oliver Fox, *Astral Projection* (New Hyde Park, New York: University Books, 1962), 32–33.
3. Herbert B. Greenhouse, *The Astral Journey* (New York: Avon Books, 1974), 4.
4. Ibid.
5. Ibid.
6. Ibid., 4–8.
7. Ibid., 9, 13.
8. Ibid., 15–16.
9. Ibid., 16–18.

CHAPTER 15   DREAMS FOR LOVE AND SEX
1. Patricia Garfield, *Creative Dreaming* (New York: Ballantine Books, 1974), 104.
2. Ibid., 104–5.

CHAPTER 25   COLORS
1. G. A. Dudley, *Dreams: Their Mysteries Revealed* (Wellingborough, Northamptonshire: The Aquarian Press, 1979), 78.
2. Ibid.
3. Ibid., 78–79.
4. Ibid., 79.
5. Ibid., 79–80.

INDEX

Thothmes IV, 40
Tibetan Book of the Dead, The, 90
Tibetan dream meditation, 63
Timeaeus (Plato), 40
Triple warmer time, 193
Twin studies, 16

UFO phenomenon, 103
Universal symbols, 25

Visionary dreams, 41, 100, 101,
    103
Vitamin B₆, 81
Voltaire, 110

Waning moon, 196, 197
Water technique, 63

Waxing moon, 196
Wellington, Duke of, 101
Whitman, Walt, 110
Wilde, Oscar, 57
Winter, 184
Wish-fulfillment dreams, 22, 23,
    25, 139
Wu Ting, 37–38

Yarrow, 78
Yin and yang, 135, 186–190, 192,
    196
Yoga, 39

Zen Buddhism, 6-7
Zeus, 38

ABOUT THE AUTHOR

Denise Linn's personal journey began as a result of a near-death experience at age seventeen. Her life-changing experiences and remarkable recovery set her on a spiritual quest that led her to explore the healing traditions of many cultures including those of her own Cherokee ancestors, the Aborigines in the Australian bush, and the Zulus in Bophuthatswana. She trained with a Hawaiian kahuna (shaman), and Reiki Master Hawayo Takata. She was also adopted into a New Zealand Maori tribe. In addition Denise lived in a Zen Buddhist monastery for over two years.

Denise is an international lecturer, healer and originator of Interior Alignment ©, and she holds regular seminars on five continents. She is the author of *Sacred Space*, *Secret Language of Signs*, and *Past Life/Present Dreams* and appears extensively on television and radio programs throughout the world. For information about her seminars and tapes write to:

Denise Linn Seminars
P.O. Box 75657
Seattle, Washington
98125-0657
USA